Always Before Me

ALWAYS BEFORE ME

90 STORY-DEVOTIONS FOR WOMEN

DAVALYNN SPENCER

Wilson Creek Publishing

Revised edition copyright 2022 by Davalynn Spencer and *Wilson Creek Publishing*
First edition copyright 2012 by Davalynn Spencer, Westbow Press

E-book ISBN 978-1-7350741-4-6
Print ISBN 978-1-7350741-5-3

All rights reserved. No part of this book may be used or reproduced by any means without the written permission of the publisher except in the case of brief quotations embodied in critical articles and reviews.

Unless otherwise indicated, all Scripture quotations are taken from the New King James Version. Copyright 1982 by Thomas Nelson, Inc. Used by permission. All rights reserved.

Scripture quotations marked NIV are taken from the Holy Bible, New International Version, NIV. Copyright 1973, 1978, 1984, 2011 by Biblica, Inc. Used by permission of Zondervan. All rights reserved worldwide. www.zondervan.com. The "NIV" and "New International Version" are trademarks registered in the United States Patent and Trademark Office by Biblica, Inc.

Scripture quotations marked MSG are taken from *THE MESSAGE*, copyright 1993, 2002, 2018 by Eugene H. Peterson. Used by permission of NavPress. All rights reserved. Represented by Tyndale House Publishers, a Division of Tyndale House Ministries.

Scripture quotations marked TLB are taken from The Living Bible copyright 1971. Used by permission of Tyndale House Publishers, Carol Stream, Illinois 60188. All rights reserved.

Wilson Creek Publishing

FOREWORD

Sometimes the smallest details, the tiniest glimpses, or the littlest moments matter the most. A sunset bursting with joy. A child sleeping in peace. A river rushing to the sea. A grandmother passing on to her heavenly home. Those moments touch your heart and stay with you. They alter your thinking. They change you.

If we'll but stop and listen.

Davalynn Spencer's story-devotionals do just that. Her life experiences help us see the Father, Son, and Holy Spirit in a new way and understand the Scriptures better. They help us slow down enough to notice those moments in our lives when the Lord is nudging us to listen, to see, to experience a lesson in our lives. To make us more like Him.

So stop, look, listen—and be transformed.

Susan G. Mathis
Former editorial director at Focus on the Family
Award-winning author of the Thousand Islands novels

PREFACE

The psalmist wrote: "I have set the LORD always before me; because He is at my right hand, I will not be moved" (Psalm 16:8). With God as his focus and companion, the psalm-singer knew he would not be shaken off his path.

As women we walk many paths: daughter, sister, wife, mother, teacher, nurse, music-maker, mourner, secretary, counselor, chauffeur, cook, lover, accountant ... the list is endless. But God knows the many things we do and He is willing to meet us in every situation.

Always Before Me is a simple observance of how God speaks to us through our daily circumstances and ordinary surroundings.

Every place we go, He has been. Every circumstance we face, He has seen. The same Voice that spoke the world into existence speaks in our hearts today, and we can hear Him if we learn to listen. We can see Him if we learn to watch.

The heartbeat of God's written Word echoes through the work of His hands. "For since the creation of the world His invisible attributes are clearly seen, being understood by the things that are made ..." (Romans 1:20). Moses encountered the great I Am in a bush that burned and a cloud that fell. Jonah recognized omnipotent God while trapped in the lightless belly of a giant fish. And a thirsty woman found the Water of Life when she met Jesus at the village well.

Each of the devotions in this revised edition are based on actual experiences in my life as wife, mother, daughter, author, teacher, and musician. The original thirty devotions are included, and with the additional sixty they provide three months of daily encouragement, Scripture, and prayer.

May these devotional thoughts encourage you to discover that a moment of insight is sometimes all it takes to find strength in the struggle.

~Davalynn Spencer

Contents

Foreword i
Preface iii
Day One: Oil in My Lamp 1
Day Two: Unleaded Bread 4
Day Three: Lot's Wife 6
Day Four: A Piece of My Mind 9
Day Five: Armored 12
Day Six: Walking in the Light 15
Day Seven: The Rest of the Story 17
Day Eight: Focus 19
Day Nine: Blessed 21
Day Ten: Shiny Shoes 23
Day Eleven: Scars 25
Day Twelve: Lift My Head 28
Day Thirteen: Enabler 31
Day Fourteen: Thinking About You 34
Day Fifteen: Eyes on Me 37
Day Sixteen: Gratitude 40
Day Seventeen: Blind to Your Blunders? 43
Day Eighteen: Trust 45
Day Nineteen: Never Too Busy 48
Day Twenty: What Rocks Your World? 51
Day Twenty-One: Veterans of Pain 53
Day Twenty-Two: Do You Hear It? 56
Day Twenty-Three: Blown Over 58
Day Twenty-Four: How Sweet Is My Grapevine? 60
Day Twenty-Five: Intentional Neglect 63
Day Twenty-Six: This Little Light 66
Day Twenty-Seven: Space Beetle 69

Day Twenty-Eight: Appearances
Can Be Deceiving 72
Day Twenty-Nine: Cutting Back 74
Day Thirty: In a Fog 76
Day Thirty-One: Am I a Name Dropper? 78
Day Thirty-Two: Boundaries:
When Enough Is More Than Enough 81
Day Thirty-Three: Give and Live 84
Day Thirty-Four: What Goes Here? 86
Day Thirty-Five: Glory 88
Day Thirty-Six: A Thousand Hills 91
Day Thirty-Seven: 93
Day Thirty-Eight: My Mother's Keeper 95
Day Thirty-Nine: Dominion 98
Day Forty: Small Talk 101
Day Forty-One: Scarred But Standing 104
Day Forty-Two: Storing the Light 106
Day Forty-Three: Oxygen 108
Day Forty-Four: Can God Forget? 110
Day Forty-Five: Mom-Care 112
Day Forty-Six: Please, Bug Me 114
Day Forty-Seven: Pour It Out 117
Day Forty-Eight: Resting in His Shadow 120
Day Forty-Nine: Scratching at
God-Knows-What 122
Day Fifty: They've Come! 124
Day Fifty-One: F.R.E.T. 126
Day Fifty-Two: F Stands for Fear 129
Day Fifty-Three: Suicide by Stubbornness 131
Day Fifty-Four: Ready, Set, Move 134
Day Fifty-Five: Peace Like a River 136
Day Fifty-Six: Out of the Storm 138
Day Fifty-Seven: Watch Your Step 140

Day Fifty-Eight: From Present to Past
and Back 142
Day Fifty-Nine: Full of It.. 145
Day Sixty: Take My Breath Away................................... 147
Day Sixty-One: A Hiding Place....................................... 149
Day Sixty-Two: Neighbors... 151
Day Sixty-Three: Life Is Unfair....................................... 153
Day Sixty-Four: Going It Alone—Or Not...................... 155
Day Sixty-Five: Perspective... 157
Day Sixty-Six: Is This Good Enough?............................ 159
Day Sixty-Seven: No Secondhand Days........................ 162
Day Sixty-Eight: Only the Clean and Unbroken:
On My Own 166
Day Seventy: Ready or Not... 168
Day Seventy-One: Out of Control 171
Day Seventy-Two: Spiritual Backbone 173
Day Seventy-Three: Procrastination............................. 175
Day Seventy-Four: The Medicine Train 178
Day Seventy-Five: Resistance... 181
Day Seventy-Six: Show, Don't Tell................................. 184
Day Seventy-Seven: Unimproved Road........................ 187
Day Seventy-Eight: TMI! 189
Day Seventy-Nine: Are Worth the Wait 191
Day Eighty: Which Voice?.. 193
Day Eighty-One: What's Your POV?.............................. 195
Day Eighty-Two: Character 198
Day Eighty-Three: The Potter 201
Day Eighty-Four: Chewing On the Bread of Life.......... 204
Day Eighty-Five: Face to Face Love............................... 206
Day Eighty-Six: Sticks and Stones and Words............ 208
Day Eighty-Seven: Windows... 211
Day Eighty-Eight: The Power of Scent......................... 213
Day Eighty-Nine: The Rock and Hard Place 216

Day Ninety: The Good Shepherd 218
Learning to Look and Listen: 220
Acknowledgments 225
About the Author 226

Day One

Oil in My Lamp

"Abide in Me and I in you."
John 15:4

*T*hunder storms roll up against Colorado's Rocky Mountains in the summer, tossing lightning along the Front Range, and often knocking out power for miles. When our children were little, I kept old-fashioned oil lamps handy for these sudden squalls. But the very first one we experienced as newcomers to the state taught me just how unprepared I really was.

One evening at dusk, the thunder crashed, our lights flickered and the power blinked out. The Arkansas River valley lay in rain-soaked stillness. Not a light shone anywhere except a paling sliver of day as it slipped behind rugged peaks in the west.

"Let's be pioneers," I said to seven-year-old Jake and three-year-old Amanda, hoping to banish their fears with a little make-believe. We gathered the kerosene lamps, bottled oil, and a package of new wicks I kept in the pantry. Confident in their mother's wisdom, my children watched as I carefully poured the precious oil into the glass lamp basins, pushed new, white cotton wicks into the burners, and screwed the burners onto the lamps.

"We have everything we need for light, just like your great-great-grandparents," I said. I struck the match and it burned down to my fingertips before I tried a second match, and then a third. Jake and Amanda stared wide-eyed at the tightly woven wick that wouldn't light no matter how many times I tried. And then they looked at me.

Fear leapt into my heart—not fear of the dark, but fear of failing my children, of not coming through on a promise. As my pulse quickened and my fingers shook, a clear understanding washed over me like the rain drenching our house. It wasn't the wick that burned, creating the light—it was the *oil in the wick* that burned. My wicks were new and dry, and it would take hours for them to soak up the oil.

By then darkness blanketed our home. I tucked my disappointed children into bed and promised that I would show them the light the next morning. Then I curled up on the sofa to watch the lightning through our picture windows.

Frustrated, I realized that my life could be just like those lamps. Even though I had everything I needed for emergency light, I hadn't prepared it. In the same way, I had every one of God's promises from His Word, but had I readied my heart by applying them? When the thunder of adversity crashed into my life, would I survive the darkness with the light of God's Word soaked up by my heart?

Jesus said, "Abide in Me, and I in you" (John 15:4). That phrase had always sounded like a paradox to me, but after I tried to light the dry wick I understood it completely. The oil couldn't get into the wick unless the wick got into the oil. And God's truth would never get into me unless I got into His Word.

The next morning I easily lit the lamp for my children, but the moment of pioneer adventure was lost. I promised myself that the next time I tried to show them the light—whether with a kerosene lamp or with my life—I would be ready.

Oh Lord, thank You for showing me what it means to abide in You. Please, pour Your life-giving oil into me as I spend time reading Your word and praying. Thank You for being there for me when the lights go out. Amen.

> "I am the light of the world. He who
> follows Me shall not walk in darkness,
> but have the light of life."
> John 8:12

Day Two

Unleaded Bread

"I am the bread of life."
John 6:35

When she was seven, our daughter, Amanda, was very proud of her understanding of communion. Growing up in the church, she had witnessed many communion services and had listened attentively as I explained that the juice represented Jesus's blood shed for our sins, and the bread or crackers represented His body broken on the cross. What I hadn't considered was the childlike filter through which she had also heard the pastor talk about unleavened bread.

One Sunday morning before the church service started, Amanda perched on her knees in the pew, visiting with a couple behind us. Listening with one ear as a mother often does when occupied elsewhere, I heard Amanda explain that unleaded bread would be served during communion.

Graciously, the couple acknowledged my daughter's explanation without laughing at her *faux pas*, and once more—through the eyes of a child—I caught a glimpse of God's perfect plan of salvation.

Unleaded, indeed! In those days, unleaded gasoline was cleaner than regular gasoline, its impurities purged away, leaving a cleaner-burning fuel. This was so similar in essence to the unleavened bread that God commanded His people to eat as part of the Passover meal, which served as the symbolic precursor of Christ's sacrificial death.

Unleavened bread represented the haste with which the Hebrews escaped Egypt's slavery; they had no time to add leaven and let the bread rise. Centuries later, Jesus condemned the "leaven of the Pharisees" (Matthew 16:6) for contaminating and spoiling the bread of life He offered.

Without knowing it, Amanda had bridged the centuries with a modern-day word picture of God's perfect grace. Whether unleavened or unleaded, what God gives us is purer, better by far.

Thank You, Lord, for continuing to teach me through the eyes and ears of a child. Amen.

> "For the bread of God
> is He who comes down from heaven
> and gives life to the world."
> John 6:33

DAY THREE

LOT'S WIFE

*"But his wife looked back behind him,
and she became a pillar of salt."*
Genesis 19:26

Colorado Highway 115 runs between Colorado Springs and the towns of Florence and Cañon City. It cuts through rocky bluffs and over cedar-dotted hills. At the southern entrance to a long canyon, a stony pillar once jutted out of the rock along the highway. The locals called it Lot's Wife, naming it for the Old Testament woman whom God punished for disobedience by turning her into a pillar of salt.

When my husband changed jobs, the move also changed my life. I had to go back to work, give up homeschooling, and send our children to public school. It was hard for me to make the change, and I kept looking back longingly at what our life had once been.

One day as I drove past Lot's Wife on my way to Colorado Springs, I thought about the rock's unchanging nature. The story in Genesis says God brought Lot's family out of a bad situation and warned them not to look back at the destruction about to follow. Lot's wife did look back, and she became a pillar of salt: immovable, unchanging, and never again able to laugh or love or live. And the example she set for her daughters produced distressing consequences. The Genesis account tells us the girls had so little faith in God that they conceived children with their father out of fear they'd never see another living man.

What consequences would result from my unwillingness to accept a change in plans? If I continued to look back and mourn the loss of our former life, what would that say to my children? If I stood frozen emotionally in time, unwilling to move forward in faith, what was I demonstrating to them about God's faithfulness?

That stony Lot's wife became for me a warning beacon and an encouragement to trust God with my family's future. My husband spent invaluable days in the next few months with our children. His daily time with them let him experience their childhood in a way he never would have enjoyed had he stayed in his earlier employment. And soon he began a new career, one that fulfilled him and demonstrated to all of us that God never forsakes us.

Lord, thank You for the warning in the story of Lot's wife. Help me be ready to go when You say go, and to stay when You say stay. Make me willing to change and grow and stretch out of my comfort zone, trusting You to provide what we need. Amen.

> "For I know the thoughts
> that I think toward you, says the Lord,
> thoughts of peace and not of evil,
> to give you a future and a hope."
> Jeremiah 29:11

Day Four

A Piece of My Mind

> "And the peace of God,
> which surpasses all understanding,
> will guard your hearts and minds
> through Christ Jesus."
> Philippians 4:7

The woman who transferred the phone call to my desk in the newsroom looked at me oddly as she said, "It's the school—about your daughter."

Amanda, a fourth grader at the time, had fallen from the monkey bars and landed face-first in the gravel. She was waiting in the principal's office for me to take her to the doctor.

As a crime-beat reporter for the local newspaper, I was accustomed to receiving bad-news phone calls—just not about my own family. I shut down my computer and gathered my purse and car keys as the woman walked over.

"I wondered how you'd act when *you* got bad news," she said smugly. "You seem to live such a charmed life. I didn't think anything ever went wrong for you."

White-hot anger shot through me, searing my tongue beyond the possibility of speech. It was a good thing, because I wanted very much to give her a piece of my mind. How dare she judge me like *that*! She didn't know that my husband had recently left his job due to stress and unrelenting pressures, creating the need for me to go to work. She didn't know about the day a dog tore into Amanda's three-year-old face, nearly ripping her nose away, or of the time our son Jake fractured his skull falling from a bicycle. How dare she say I lived a charmed life!

On my way to the school, the Lord gently pointed out that it wasn't a piece of my mind the fellow employee needed, it was the *peace* of my mind. She knew I professed to be a Christian. She saw me navigate on-the-job snags every day, but she wanted to know if the steady surface stream ran deeper. Would calm prevail when the phone call was more personal, or would an emotional torrent overflow the banks in a flood of hysteria?

She and I talked later about Amanda's accident and recovery. I tried to explain that the Lord cares for us even in the hard or disappointing times, but I felt the pressure as I left the conversation, knowing that she was watching closely.

I knew that sooner or later I would fail to exhibit the peace God gives. Someday I would substitute my own panic and fear. But I couldn't live my life for performance's sake; I had to trust God to get me through the tough times and pray that His peace would eventually show through the cracks in my life.

Thank You, Lord, for helping me pass that test of observation—I've failed so many others! Help me remember that people really are reading my life as a living love letter from You. Thank You, Lord, for caring that much.

> "You are an epistle of Christ, ministered by us,
> written not with ink
> but by the Spirit of the living God,
> not on tablets of stone but on tablets of flesh,
> that is, of the heart."
> 2 Corinthians 3:3

DAY FIVE

ARMORED

> "Put on the whole armor of God,
> that you may be able to stand against
> the wiles of the devil."
> Ephesians 6:11

When my husband went into law enforcement as his second career, the old adage of always being prepared took on new meaning. He was on duty even when he wasn't on duty. If his pager sounded in the middle of the night, he would grab his protective vest, gun, and duty belt, rush out the door, and speed away into the dark.

He never went anywhere unprepared. Others may have not realized it, but he was always armed, always ready. When I asked him why, he said, "How would people feel if something happened and they looked to me for help or protection, and I wasn't prepared?"

I marveled at the parallel between my husband's job and our responsibility as Christians. We are told to always be ready to give a reason for our hope to those who ask (1 Peter 3:15). And Jesus warned us to watch, for we don't know the hour or day of His return (Matthew 25:13).

I marveled too at the parallel between the armor of God and the gear my husband wore on duty:

THE BELT OF TRUTH:
> His duty belt held everything together. It carried his gun, handcuffs, radio, and other equipment—everything close at hand.

THE BREASTPLATE OF RIGHTEOUSNESS:
> His bullet-resistant vest covered his heart, lungs, and other vital organs.

THE SHOES OF THE GOSPEL OF PEACE:
> He was a peace officer, sent to walk the streets for the safety and protection of the people.

THE SHIELD OF FAITH:
> His badge, often called a shield, gave him the authority to stop the bad guys.

THE HELMET OF SALVATION:
> His hat identified his affiliation, those for whom he worked.

THE SWORD OF THE SPIRIT:
> His gun was the weapon, the one piece of his uniform that was offensive rather than defensive.

Altogether, my husband's uniform enabled him to stand safely against the scheming of those who chose to kill, steal, and destroy—as does the armor Jesus has prepared for me.

Will I take the time to put it on?

Lord, thank You for arming us for spiritual battle, not sending us out unprotected. Help me not to forget that I really am in a battle for the souls of those around me. Amen.

> "But let us who are of the day be sober,
> putting on the breastplate of faith and love,
> and as a helmet the hope of salvation."
> 1 Thessalonians 5:8

Day Six

Walking in the Light

"Indeed, the darkness shall not hide from You,
But the night shines as the day;
the darkness and the light are both alike to You."
Psalm 139:12

When my husband and I were first married, we had a two-in-one flashlight. It was equipped with the standard high-beam light that shone from one end like most models, but it also had a softer, more radiant light that spread from a second bulb along the top.

One evening I took the flashlight outside for a trek to the barn. The standard beam lit the path ahead, punching through the dark toward my destination. I switched to the second light and it illuminated my steps and the area right around me, spreading into the shadows on either side. But I couldn't have both lights on at the same time. I had to choose one or the other.

As I walked, a familiar verse from the Psalms came to mind: "Your word is a lamp to my feet and a light for my path" (Psalm 119:105). Suddenly, I understood the metaphor.

God's wisdom shows me the path ahead as well as the ground beneath my feet. It is not limited like my hand-held flashlight that required an either-or choice. His Word sheds the light of understanding in both ways at the same time. His Word is indeed a lamp to my feet *and* a light to my path.

The Psalms also tell us, "You, LORD, keep my lamp burning; my God turns my darkness into light" (Psalm 18:28 NIV).

That's exactly what I need in this life of unforeseen obstacles and sudden shadows—a never-failing power source that faithfully shows me the way to go and how to get there.

The Lord's light cuts through my darkness, and the lamp of His love envelops me with the comfort of His presence.

Thank You, Lord, that there is no darkness in You, that Your light directs our steps. Amen.

> "Your word is a lamp to my feet
> and a light for my path."
> Psalm 119:105

Day Seven

The Rest of the Story

"Come to Me, all you who labor
and are heavy laden, and I will give you rest."
Matthew 11:28

"Rest. Oh God, I need rest."
I'll give you rest.
"Really?"
You're tired, overloaded.
"No kidding."
Come to Me.
"Okay."
Here, put this on.
"Wait a minute—"
It's Mine; try it.
"But this is a—"
Learn from Me.
"Learn what?"
Undemanding gentleness and humility.
"But doesn't this mean more work?"
It is soul-rest.
"I could use that."
Put it on; I'll be right beside you.

"But it's a yoke."
My burden is light.
"Light?"
I am the Light of the world.
"I see."
You will.

Oh God, I need Your help to rest in You, to trust You to be in control, leading me. To *let* you lead me. Thank You for Your patience and staying power. Amen.

> "Take my yoke upon you and learn from Me,
> for I am gentle and lowly in heart,
> and you will find rest for your souls."
> Matthew 11:29

Day Eight

Focus

> "And when he saw that the wind was boisterous, he was afraid."
> Matthew 14:30

As a reporter and photographer for a daily newspaper in southern Colorado, I often used a long lens on my camera for distance shots, a lens that would get me into the picture without getting me into the action. I have photographed Rocky Mountain big horn sheep in the wild, house windows exploding into flames, police apprehending an armed fugitive, even a First Lady during her visit to a Denver bookstore.

The selling point of a telephoto lens is the way it cuts everything out of the picture and zooms in on the focus of your aim. The subject is drawn in, enlarged, and defined within the camera's viewfinder. Everything around it blurs or disappears.

My spiritual life is a lot like a telephoto lens. As long as I keep my eyes on Jesus, I'm not distracted by countless other things demanding my attention, drawing me away from my focus. There always seems to be something that tries to snag my concentration—

like the waves that drew Peter's eyes away from Jesus. When Peter lost his focus and reacted to his threatening surroundings, he began to sink. But the Lord in mercy and understanding reached out and kept Peter from drowning.

Thank God, He does the same for me! For I am still learning that when I keep the Lord in my spiritual viewfinder, I'm not sidetracked or discouraged. Regardless of the surrounding temptations or challenges, if He is the focus of my vision, I can walk in peace rather than fear.

Lord, help me keep You in my sights and keep my sights focused on You. There are so many distractions screaming for my attention. Be my goal. Amen.

> "Looking unto Jesus, the author
> and finisher of our faith,
> who for the joy that was set before Him
> endured the cross—"
> Hebrews 12:2

Day Nine

Blessed

"Her children rise up and call her blessed."
Proverbs 31:28

I was with my oldest sister when she died. So were her daughter and six sons. Never before had I seen a bunch of grown men weep like little boys.

As the youngest of five, I was born eighteen years after my sister, Janis. Her children had been more than niece and nephews to me—they were playmates. The day she succumbed to lung cancer, at home by her request, we all stood around her bed, children again. I had seen these men cry as boys after fistfights or consumed by juvenile jealousy. But that day they wept for the one woman in their lives who had shown them unconditional love. In the few hours she lingered with us, I saw reflected in their faces and in their touch the tenderness she had shown to them over scraped knees and broken toys. Now their hearts broke in helplessness, forced to let her go without being able to do anything about it.

Three of the sons and the daughter were my sister's stepchildren, brought into her life by a loving husband and father with whom she shared nearly thirty years. There was no difference in their tears, their grief. All were her children, and they knew it. She had spent her life telling them.

We will all say good-bye to our children, whether face-to-face or not, only God knows. And we will reap what we have sown into their hearts. My sister gathered the rewards of love planted year after year in faithfulness. Her family was not perfect; they struggled through hard times and disappointments. They argued and anguished just like everyone else. But through it all ran the cord of her love, and in her dying moments the greatest eulogy of her life was written on the faces of her children.

Oh Lord, may my love for my children be a thread that runs strong through their lives, binding them to each other and to You. Amen.

> "Give her of the fruit of her hands,
> And let her own works praise her in the gates."
> Proverbs 31:31

Day Ten

Shiny Shoes

"For I will contend with him who contends with you,
And I will save your children."
Isaiah 49:25

The man with the shiny black shoes sat down on our living room sofa and told us why the US Army was a great career choice for our son. Jake was about to graduate from high school, and he had met the Army recruiter at a career day at school. Two short years of his life and he would be trained for the military as well as a career in the field of his choice, Shiny Shoes promised.

I felt like I was losing control, but of what? This man had come into our home and, in so many words, told me he was going to take my son away. I resented his presence, but I knew Jake was supposed to grow up and go out on his own. That's what his father and I had raised him to do. I guess I didn't expect it to happen so suddenly. Eighteen years just isn't very long when you're in the eighteenth year.

It could be a lot worse, I told myself, watching the yellow lamplight shimmer on the black patent-leather shoes. Some parents lose their children to tragic accidents or drugs or reckless living or any number of things. The Army offered self-discipline, direction, determination. Yes, it could be worse.

It was the letting go that was hard. Every day up to that point had been preparation for letting go, yet I was still frightened. Why was it so much easier to trust God with my own life than to trust Him with my children? Maybe the issue was not trusting God, but trusting them, which meant I had to trust God even more.

The last pair of shiny black shoes I had seen were on my own ten-year-old feet swinging above the floor from the church pew where I sat with my parents. The next pair I saw would likely be on my son at boot camp on graduation day. Life is short, isn't it?

Thank You, Lord, that I can trust You with my children. Thank You for the comfort of knowing that You go with them to places I'll never be able to go. You help them in ways I never could. Help me remember that You are in control and I am not. I'm so glad. Amen.

> "I do not pray that
> You should take them out of the world,
> but that You should keep them from the evil one."
> John 17:15

Day Eleven

Scars

"See, I have inscribed you
on the palms of My hands."
Isaiah 49:16

Carpal tunnel surgery left an inch-long scar on the heel of my right hand. For weeks I held the tender area flat against my body while in public or at church, instead offering my left hand when greeting people.
As it healed, I cautiously ventured back into my normal activities: writing, cooking, playing the piano, and teaching. But I tended to hide the ugly pink scar that cut across from wrist to palm. Exposing it made me feel vulnerable to possible pain or injury, even rejection from others.

On Sundays I felt self-conscious about raising my hand during worship—a common practice for many who attended our church. What if someone turned and looked at that imperfect hand? How could I lift it up to a perfect God? I was embarrassed.

And then one Sunday morning the worship music touched my heart so deeply that I had to raise my hand. I suddenly felt bare, exposed, as if I were lifting my whole imperfect, scarred life to God. Would He accept me?

In that moment I sensed Him reaching down to me through the scarred hands of Jesus. It was as if He were revealing His own wounds, opening His hands to me, unhesitatingly, unembarrassed. I realized that I was not the only one who had scars in her hands. Nor was I the only one with scars on her heart. Isn't that all we really have to offer God anyway—our torn, ruined lives?

The apostle Paul said, "I bear in my body the marks of the Lord Jesus" (Galations 6:17). I always wondered what he meant by that. Was he referring to the physical beatings he suffered for the sake of his faith, or was he speaking metaphorically about spiritual scars? Either way, my light discomfort was not to be compared with Christ's torturous suffering, yet I couldn't help but think of the scars of Jesus when I looked at my own. The wounds in His hands perhaps were similar, though not neatly stitched together like mine. They gaped, no doubt, from the weight of His body hanging on the cross, and the weight of my sins on his heart.

After the resurrection, Jesus offered His scar-torn hands to a doubting man named Thomas and told him to put his finger in the holes to see that they were real. Could I say that to someone? Was I willing to share my hidden wounds and shame with others so they too could believe and be healed?

Thank You, Lord, for reaching out to me. Thank You for the scars of Your love. Amen.

"But He was wounded for our transgression."
Isaiah 53:5

Day Twelve

Lift My Head

"But You, O LORD, are a shield for me,
my glory and the One who lifts up my head."
Psalm 3:3

As evening slipped down the pale green walls of our son's hospital room, I shifted in the plastic chair and watched Jake's eighteen-year-old body fight to heal itself. I was angry.

A week earlier, Jake had wrecked a friend's motorcycle on a gravel road near our home in southern Colorado. The friend hadn't come to see him; neither did the boy's parents. No phone calls, no cards. The disregard cut deeply, and I clung to my anger as tenaciously as Jake clung to his life.

In the emergency room the night of the accident, Jake had cried out to his father and me to lift his head. "Just for a minute, Mom. Please, lift my head!" EMTs at the scene had taped his head to a body board to stabilize his neck. Unknown to the doctors who refused to medicate him for fear of masking injuries or symptoms, the tape pressed Jake's skull to the board against a gaping wound. Jake's cries pierced my heart. I longed to cut the tape and lift his head, but I knew it could result in paralysis.

Due to summer thunderstorms that downed the Flight for Life helicopters, we waited three hours for a mobile trauma unit from the Pueblo hospital thirty-five miles away.

Gravel pitted Jake's back, hips, and face. The accident had cost him his right eyebrow, fractured his skull, and shut down his kidneys. He was nauseated, delirious, stubborn, hateful, forgetful—all common with a head injury, doctors said. For three weeks my husband and I took turns staying with him. We couldn't leave him alone. My anger grew.

As I tried to sleep on the chair in Jake's room that night, Jesus spoke to me—not audibly, but undoubtedly. "You have only two hands," He said. "You cannot hang on to Jake and your anger and Me. Of which will you let go?"

God knew I was angry. He knew I hurt more than I had ever hurt. But He also knew that if I clung to the anger, it would destroy me and maybe even my son.

I willed myself to let it go and placed my hand in Jesus's hand that night. I would not let go of Jake, and I could not go through the ordeal without God's help.

The words of a song based on Psalm 3 became my unending prayer, that the Lord would be a shield for Jake and the lifter of his head. Only God could keep him alive and heal his injuries.

Jake recovered quickly, and the neurosurgeon released him earlier than expected. Light-headedness bothered him at first, but with time, even that disappeared. The Lord indeed lifted his head—and mine from the death-like grip of anger.

O Lord, thank You for taking me through the hard places, for showing me what my anger would cost, and for loving me enough to make me confront it. Oh God, thank You for Your forgiveness and mercy and for helping me pass it on to others.

> "You who lift me up from the gates of death … I will rejoice in Your salvation."
> Psalm 9:13-14

Day Thirteen

Enabler

> "A word fitly spoken is like
> apples of gold in settings of silver."
> Proverbs 25:11

A woman from church encouraged me that God had equipped me to accomplish certain tasks that lay ahead.

She referred to the "apples of gold" in Proverbs 25:11. Her words were exactly what I needed to hear.

I munched on that golden apple, relishing the taste of knowing God had prepared me, and I thanked Him for enabling me.

Social norms immediately swept through my mind, denouncing my use of the term *enabling,* but I resisted the taint associated with the word.

Merriam-Webster lists the following definition for **Enable: 1 a:** to provide with the means or opportunity … **b:** to make possible, practical, or easy … **c:** to cause to operate … **2:** to give legal power, capacity, or sanction to.[1]

The next entry in the *MW* dictionary adds an *r* to the end of *enable* and the word becomes *enabler*, the less-than-flattering term that today bears a load of negative connotations.

Again, I resisted. God enables us but not in a passively harmful way. He empowers us, strengthens us, gives us what we need to serve Him and grow in faith.

One morning soon after, my devotional reading took me to John 6 and the account of people deserting Jesus because of something He'd said. He explained to His disciples that He knew even some of them didn't really believe, and added:

"This is why I told you that no one can come to me unless the Father has enabled him." (John 6:65 NIV)

Though surprised to see that the translation used the word *enable,* I was thrilled to find it. I felt vindicated somehow.

Of course God enables us. How else would we have strength for anything?

The choice is ours, but the power is His.

Oh God of all strength and grace, thank You for enabling me. Thank You for giving me Your gifts and empowering me to use them. May I always use them for Your glory. Amen.

"For it is God who works in you
both to will and to do for His good pleasure."
Philippians 2:13

[1] *Merriam-Webster.com Dictionary,* s.v. "enable," accessed March 21, 2022, https://www.merriam-webster.com/dictionary/enable.

Day Fourteen

Thinking About You

> "Delight yourself also in the LORD,
> And He shall give you the desires of your heart."
> Psalm 37:4

Mary Beth's high school friend had a very handsome brother named David. He didn't pay much attention to Mary Beth because she was four years younger and he was a college man. But sometimes when she visited her friend, she got to see David too.

When David was a senior at Clairemont Graduate School in Southern California, he asked Mary Beth to a ball game and later to a concert. David was everything Mary Beth had hoped for in a husband, with one crucial exception: he was not a Christian.

After high school, Mary Beth attended Westmont College and there met a young man preparing for the ministry who asked her to marry him.

"One day my mother came up to visit. She said she had talked to David's mother and he'd become a Christian. That's when I knew I was engaged to the wrong fellow."

Mary Beth prayed about what to do, gave the young preacher's ring back, and left school at mid-semester.

"I hadn't been home two weeks and the phone rang and it was *this* gentleman," Mary Beth said, reaching across her dining room table fifty-two years later to take his hand. Between the two of them sat a bouquet of lilies and pink carnations commemorating the recent anniversary of their wedding day.

"How did you know?" David asked her, as if for the first time.

"Because I was thinking about *you*," she said. "I couldn't marry him when I was thinking about you."

My neighbor Mary Beth was focused on the love of her life and she didn't mind waiting. The hardest test no doubt was saying no to that love before he'd met Christ. But she could say no because Christ was bigger in her heart than even David. Because she waited, she reaped more than half a century of love in a world where couples break up at the slightest tempest.

Our thoughts direct our lives for better or worse. Jesus said we speak from "the abundance of the heart" (Luke 6:45). Today we call that abundance our thought life. Our reading and viewing habits are critical. We are literally filling our inner reservoirs through the openings of our eyes and ears. Like computers, what goes into our minds is what comes out.

Mary Beth knew what a difference the focus of her thinking could make. It changed the course of her life.

Lord, help me focus my thoughts on You by filling my inner reservoir from Your Word and spending time with Your children. Thank You for giving me the direction I need to live a life pleasing to You. Amen.

> "For as he thinks in his heart, so is he."
> Proverbs 23:7

Day Fifteen

Eyes on Me

> "It shall come to pass that before they call,
> I will answer;
> and while they are still speaking,
> I will hear."
> Isaiah 65:24

*I*t's that personal word that hits the mark—when someone speaks to you directly about what's been bothering you. That's when you feel like your problem is important, that *you* are important, and that someone cares.

Nothing else compares with this, and when I am afraid (of age, financial need, lack of direction, death of a dream, my children's choices), it is exactly what I need.

My fears found me on the living room sofa, next to the window, with my morning cup of hot honeyed tea. A night of fitful sleep, hovering what-ifs, and discouraging doubts had left me worn and worried. I opened my Bible to Psalm 79, the next on my list to read.

> "May your mercy come quickly to meet us,
> for we are in desperate need." (v.8 NIV)

Stunned, I read these words as if they were mine. How could the writer have known so many years ago what my own heart would cry out today?

Surely a coincidence, I thought as I turned to the next book I'd committed to read and pulled the pages back to where my marker lay in chapter 26.

"Not today, Isaiah, please. No ranting today," I pleaded. As if I could actually speak to the man who had told ancient Israel their unfaithfulness would lead to captivity.

"You will keep in perfect peace
those whose minds are steadfast,
because they trust in you. Trust in the Lord forever,
for the Lord, the Lord himself, is the Rock eternal."
(vv.3-4NIV)

Oh, Isaiah! What words of comfort, when for so many days you've had nothing but rebuke!

Coincidence again? That both of these ancient writers would touch on such specific points that matched my pain?

As is my habit, I went to the piano to play through a few favorite songs, keeping my fingers limber and my memory fresh with their melodies. From where I had stopped the day before, I turned to the next song, "A Mighty Fortress." Several measures in, I sang out that I would keep my eyes on the Lord. I thought of Peter on the water, how he walked on the waves for a moment.

The next song, "Still," surprised me with its pointed declaration that I could soar with God above a stormy sea and roaring thunder.

Okay, God. I get it. No coincidence.

Could it get more personal than this, that He would touch my heart with both His Word and song? Did I really believe in coincidence where my heart was concerned? Did I really think my tears went unseen and my prayers unheard?

And suddenly, simply, deep within my sense of knowing, I saw Jesus looking right at me and smiling.

"Keep your eyes on Me," He said.

He had found me in the waves. Right where I needed Him, He had found me, lifted me up, and set me on my way again. With hope and the sweet intimacy of His peace.

Because of Your specific, personal promise, oh God, I will make it. Thank You. Amen.

> "You know my sitting down and my rising up;
> You understand my thought afar off. ...
> For there is not a word on my tongue, but behold,
> O Lord, You know it altogether."
> Psalm 139:2–4

Day Sixteen

Gratitude

*"And having food and clothing,
with these we shall be content."*
1 Timothy 6:8

The year my family returned to California, we moved in with my recently widowed mother-in-law, who suffered from an eye condition known as macular degeneration. A retired elementary school teacher who always had a pleasant word for everyone, she graciously opened her home, thankful that we had come to take care of her.

After twenty-seven years in my own marriage, the move was an adventure in sojourning to say the least. I was living somewhere temporarily, like Moses in the land of Midian or Jacob in Egypt. And though I loved my mother-in-law dearly, I still felt that I was in *her* house, with *her* dishes, *her* rugs on the floor, *her* pictures on the walls, and *her* furniture. I knew it was temporary, but oh, how I longed for a home of my own.

One morning, sitting at the kitchen table before anyone else got up, I replayed my repetitious prayer for a home of my own. Yes, God had provided everything we needed. He had helped us make the interstate move, and we were serving Him as we cared for a family member, but I felt like a lost child, an outsider, and an orphan.

It was then the Holy Spirit opened my eyes to my self-centeredness and showed me how to focus instead on gratitude. Had my former home really been mine the last twelve years, or was it the Lord's? Had I not been just a steward there, taking care of the things He put in my custody? Why should it be any different now?

I looked at the Early American maple kitchen table and said, "Thank You, Lord, for this table." It represented the food He provided for my family. I looked up at the vaulted, beamed ceiling and said, "Thank You, Lord, for this roof." It covered my children and kept the rain out and the warmth in. Finally, thinking of a recent, restful night's sleep, I said, "Thank You, Lord, for this bed," for it represented His faithfulness every night (see Psalm 92:2).

Today, several years later in my own home, those simple phrases come to my rescue when I start complaining about this or that needed repair, or some out-of-style décor I can't afford to change: "Thank You, Lord, for this table, this roof, and this bed. You have given me everything I need."

It all belongs to Him, and a grateful heart helps me remember that.

Whatever table, roof, and bed You choose to provide, they are the right ones for me, Lord. Thank You, for I know they come from Your loving hand. Amen.

Davalynn Spencer

"In everything give thanks;
for this is the will of God in Christ Jesus for you."
1 Thessalonians 5:18

Day Seventeen

Blind to Your Blunders?

"Who can understand his errors?"
Psalm 19:12

*H*ave you ever re-read an email—after you sent it—and discovered a mistake? How about a letter, résumé, or even a text message?

Ouch.

I moonlight as a proofreader. As such, I find mistakes in other people's writing. Typos, misspellings, grammar gaffes. The job isn't that difficult if one knows the rules. I mean, really—don't we all easily see the mistakes of others? Getting paid to do so is the trick.

However, finding my own errors isn't quite so easy. That's because I already know what I wanted to say. Therefore, when I read what I've written, my brain "sees" what I meant, not what I actually wrote.

Because of my part-time occupation as a fault-finder (doesn't sound as nice as *proofreader*, does it?) I was thrilled one morning this week when I found scriptural support for my work. I may even use the verse as a personal tagline:

"Who can understand his errors?"

Yes! Validation for proofreaders everywhere!

While the line may be a catchy phrase for a business card, there is much more to the message. It's a prayer:

"Cleanse me from secret faults."

That's exactly what I need—forgiveness as well as fresh air. I don't want to harbor those secret sins because eventually they'll ferment and overflow and stain every good thing I've ever done.

Who knows my hidden faults better than our loving Lord? Who better to handle them and make me clean through and through?

I'm so grateful for God's discerning eye on the story of my life. That story will be better, stronger, and sweeter if I allow His cleansing edit.

The question is, will I accept His loving critique, or insist on doing things my way?

Oh God of perfection, thank You for being patient with me. For giving me the help of Your Holy Spirit to make the changes You want to see in my life. Amen.

> "Keep back Your servant
> also from presumptuous sins;
> Let them not have dominion over me."
> Psalm 19:13

DAY EIGHTEEN

TRUST

> "Trust in the LORD with all your heart,
> and lean not on your own understanding;
> In all your ways acknowledge Him,
> and He shall direct your paths."
> Proverbs 3:5–6

*"B*ut God, I don't want to *trust* You, I want to *know*!"

As I bounced along in the back seat of our realtor's Jeep, I recalled how comical that confession had sounded on the lips of a Bible study leader years ago. Now I shared it completely as the Jeep pressed on past oak trees, over a rock-lined creek, and up the side of a mountain. Alone in the back seat, I hung on and prayed: *Lord, I want to know – how bad does this road get?*

We followed what must have once been a cow path that corkscrewed itself around the side of the hill.

Does it get any worse than this, Lord? The curves were so steep and sudden, I couldn't see much farther ahead than the front of the car. What if there were other vehicles headed our way on a blind collision course? What if we were forced over the edge? Who in their right mind would buy a house up here? My grip on the back seat tightened.

And then we were there. About three hundred feet above the valley floor, the hilltop leveled off with shade trees, a home, and rose bushes. But that wasn't what took my breath away. When we stepped out of the Jeep and around the corner of the house, there it was—the *view*.

Below me spread the eastern end of a ranch-land valley. A creek ambled past several ponds, oak-covered foothills rolled gently up on the left, and the snowy peaks of the Sierra Nevada strutted above them to the south. Four or five miles west, Lake Success Reservoir glistened in the afternoon sun, cupped like a drink of cool water between sun-browned hands. And the clear, blue sky capped it all with breathless beauty. I was speechless.

We lived several years on that hilltop, and the ride up quickly became commonplace. It was the same road, the same hill, the same me, but with a big difference: I knew what was coming. I knew I could make it up, around, and over the top because I had done it before. The first time terrified me because I had to trust the driver to get me through unfamiliar territory.

I prefer familiarity to faith. I like it when I know what's coming. And I'd really rather do the driving myself. But God asks me to trust Him, and that's what makes my faith grow.

God asks me to go where He leads, even if I can't see around the next corner. He asks me to keep pushing ahead, even if the road drops off next to me in a sheer cliff. He asks me to trust Him to drive me to the top. And once we make it, He always has something waiting for me that takes my breath away.

Thank You, Lord, for helping me trust You. It is so worth it. Help me trust you more. Amen.

> "But without faith it is impossible to please Him,
> for he who comes to God must believe that He is,
> and that He is a rewarder of those
> who diligently seek Him."
> Hebrews 11:6

Day Nineteen

Never Too Busy

> "Then little children were brought to Him
> that He might put His hands on them and pray,
> but the disciples rebuked them. But Jesus said,
> 'Let the little children come to Me,
> and do not forbid them;
> for of such is the kingdom of heaven.'"
> Matthew 19:13–14

Searching for just the right groundcover to plant on our hillside, I stopped by our local nursery. A big man with an even bigger straw hat, dark glasses, and full sleeve tattoos led me out to a lattice-covered patio toward several varieties of drought-resistant plants. As he pointed out the ice plant and aptenia, a small boy peddled his bike down the path between the perennials and stopped to visit. Straw Hat Man didn't ignore the boy, but called him by name and greeted him cheerfully, all the while continuing to wait on me, his paying customer. I chose two flats of red apple aptenia, and we walked back inside the main building toward the section of environmentally safe insecticides.

"Look at my new bike seat that my dad bought for me," the little boy said proudly as he followed us inside. Straw Hat Man took a moment to look at the gray-and-white camouflage-patterned seat and commented approvingly. Then he pointed out a bottle of anti-dog and cat spray to keep my ever-digging puppy out of the new plantings and something to kill ants that wouldn't also kill the cats.

I couldn't help but notice the way the man acknowledged the little boy while helping me with my purchases. He never brushed him off, ignored him, or spoke a harsh, impatient word. And the child seemed comfortable around him, as though riding his bike into the store to see Straw Hat Man was a daily ritual. Somehow it made me feel welcome too.

As I paid my bill, the nursery owner walked up and moved the boy's bike from the middle of the aisle where he'd left it.

"People might run into your bike if you leave it here," he said, leaning it against the checkout counter. "People like me," he added with a smile.

I don't know who the little boy was, but I learned a lot about the nursery owner and Straw Hat Man that day from the way they treated him. No doubt that little guy felt a certain amount of self-worth in the way he was welcomed at the nursery—so much so that he wasn't afraid to come right in.

Oh Lord, help me keep an open heart to people who "intrude" on my life when I'm busy—whether they are my own children, my husband, or a stranger who may just need a friendly greeting. You weren't too busy to bless the children, Jesus. Help me do the same. Amen.

> "And whoever receives one little child like this in My name receives Me."
> Matthew 18:5

Day Twenty

What Rocks Your World?

> "For who is God, except the Lord?
> And who is a rock, except our God?"
> Psalm 18:31

*I*t started with an antique canister in the kitchen and the tinny tune it played as it rattled back and forth.

Why was it moving?

Soon, other canisters joined in the song. Then the cupboard doors, framed pictures on a shelf, and a deep rumbling beneath my feet.

Earthquake.

Within twenty minutes, two smaller temblors struck, shaking our hilltop home, reminding me that this world is on shaky footing at best. However, the hands that hold it are steady as a rock.

"The Lord is my rock," wrote the psalmist (Psalm 18:2).

It's difficult to picture a rock as comforting, but Scripture frequently uses the metaphor to help us understand a spiritual principle.

Isaiah wrote of "the shadow of a great rock in a thirsty land" (Isaiah 32:2). I can't help but envision a treeless plain with no refuge in sight—until a weary soul stumbles upon a rock big enough to offer shade from a blazing sun or shelter from a blistering sandstorm.

Again, the psalmist wrote, "Lead me to the rock that is higher than I" (Psalm 61:2b). That is exactly what I want when I'm in need—something, Someone bigger than me.

When Moses asked to see the glory of God, the Almighty said to him, "There is a place near me where you may stand on a rock … I will put you in a cleft in the rock and cover you with my hand until I have passed by (Exodus 33:21–22 NIV).

That's where I want to be—a place near God where I can stand on a rock while He hides me with His hand.

How grateful I am that He is that close, that He is the shade that protects me from the heat of oppression and the wind of torment. That He is immovable and unshakable when my world is rocked.

Whether earthquake or soul-quaking news, I'm so glad that Jesus is my Rock.

Thank You, Lord, that when my world is rocked, You are my solid foundation. Amen.

> "The Lord is my rock and my fortress
> and my deliverer;
> my God, my strength, in whom I will trust;
> my shield and the horn of my salvation,
> my stronghold."
> Psalm 18:2

Day Twenty-One

Veterans of Pain

*"If I ascend into heaven, You are there;
If I make my bed in hell, behold, You are there."*
Psalm 139:8

After two days of excruciating pain and two more of mind-numbing drugs, I learned several things.

1. It is not wise to ignore new, inexplicable pain—it's trying to tell you something.
2. I can walk and work more slowly and the world will not fall off its axis.
3. Breakfast in bed is not all it's cracked up to be.
4. And if that bed is "in the depths," God is still there.

Many of us do more than we should and need to cut back on what we consider absolute responsibility. It's hard. It's guilt-laden. It's worse if no one else is taking care of the problem, for then we feel obligated to jump in and fix it.

Let me clarify that: *I* feel obligated …

But when it comes to cutting back, I have recently learned that *everything* can be cut back and life does not come to an end.

I have not yet heard the grinding of earth's gears slowing because I didn't get everything on my to-do list completed when, where, and how I thought they should be.

Getting sick was not on that list, but as hour after hour piled up more and more unfinished tasks and beautifully orchestrated expectations, I was forced to let go of each and every one, lie back in the arms of the Lord, and let Him carry me.

Again, hard to do.

Again, He was there, as always. And I realized that He is a veteran of pain.

In recent years, we have thought of battle fields and enemy armies when we hear the word *veteran*, as well we should. Those men and women are deserving of our respect, gratitude, and prayers.

But there is also silent suffering of which we may not be aware. The veterans who know that God is there, even in the grip of ongoing pain and disease, even when they don't understand the whys of their situations.

I once heard the mother of one such sufferer say with deep conviction, "Oh, our God, we do not know what to do, but our eyes are upon You."

Is there any better place to fix our gaze?

Indeed, Lord, our eyes are upon You. Thank You for walking with us through every valley, not just the pleasant places, but also the deep dark places of pain. Amen.

"For we have no power against
this great multitude that is coming against us;
nor do we know what to do,
but our eyes are upon You."
2 Chronicles 20:12

Day Twenty-Two

Do You Hear It?

> "And He said to them, 'Come aside by yourselves to a deserted place and rest a while.'"
> Mark 6:31

Just before the sun climbs Hatchet Peak behind our house, songbirds announce the pending dawn and cows call their calves from grassy beds.

Such a chorus greets me each summer morning that I walk. It's an hour unlike any other—cool, for one thing, not yet drenched in the greater San Joaquin Valley's triple-digit heat.

Campbell Creek meanders through the lower ranchland, past massive oaks and shady willows. Bullfrogs bay from their pond-side hideaways, and I imagine the unusual cacophony as a chorus of praise, wondering if God understands the language of His creation better than we do.

"Give thanks to the Lord," trills the high-pitched voice of a red-winged blackbird.

"His love endures forever," drums a deep-throated bullfrog.

Could it be that we humans don't take time to listen to the song of nature around us?

Could it be that we are missing out on creation's ultimate worship music?

But what if you live in the city? What if you can't walk where there is no traffic to clutter your eyes and ears and lungs? What if all you hear is the noise of people and their busy-ness?

Then find a place.

Find a place in the bedroom with the door closed and no sounds coming through. Find a place on the living room sofa while the kids are outside playing.

Hide in the bathroom if you must. I have a friend who does.

Go to the park, sit in the backyard in the shade, drive to the country in the evening after sunset, but wherever you go, quiet yourself and listen. And see if you can hear an anthem of praise, whether it is the voice of nature, the song of silence, or the simple offering of your own grateful heart.

Worship Him, and let His presence surround you.

Oh Lord, You know how hard it can be to find a quiet place. Help me. Show me where I can go to meet with You. Amen.

> "You will show me the path of life;
> In Your presence is fullness of joy;
> At Your right hand are pleasures forevermore."
> Psalm 16:11

Day Twenty-Three

Blown Over

> "Serving only themselves ... they are ...
> late autumn trees without fruit,
> twice dead, pulled up by the roots."
> Jude 1:12

The wind had been blowing so hard that we didn't hear the tree fall. It wasn't until later, after the rain subsided, that I walked outside in the dark and sensed a new openness. A tall, fruitless mulberry tree had stood at the east end of our long, covered porch. Now there was nothing.

I stepped out into the yard and found the house undamaged. The tree had simply fallen over, and it rested on the lawn like a dead, rootless fence post.

The massive head of leafy branches needed the strength of a spreading root system, yet there were no roots at all on the south side of the tree from which the storm had come. It had grown at the edge of our hilltop, with shallow, lopsided roots, and had nothing with which to grab the earth when the wind blew from that fatal direction.

How like that tree I could be—ready for almost anything, except the wind that whips up from the south when I'm not looking. Then *wham*, I'm down.

The apostle Paul warned believers to establish a good foundation for their faith, to learn everything they could about God and His great care for them. "Let your roots go down deep into the soil of God's marvelous love," he wrote to the Ephesians (3:17 TLB). Today his words still encourage us to be "rooted and grounded" so we can begin to understand God's immeasurable love and goodness.

It's all about being prepared *before* the wind starts blowing. And it will blow, we can be sure of that.

Lord, help me send my roots down into the rich soil of Your love by spending time in Your Word and in prayer. Help me grow strong in You so I can withstand the winds that tear through my life. Thank You for giving me food and water that feed my soul and strengthen my life in You. Amen.

> "As you have therefore received
> Christ Jesus the Lord,
> so walk in Him, rooted and built up in Him
> and established in the faith,
> as you have been taught,
> abounding in it with thanksgiving."
> Colossians 2:6–7

DAY TWENTY-FOUR

HOW SWEET IS MY GRAPEVINE?

"Let your speech always be with grace."
Colossians 4:6

I recently received a reply to an email, and it packed quite a surprise.

"I forwarded your e-mail on to ..."

Oops. I intended that correspondence for the recipient's eyes only.

Too late. Tap the "send" button and it's just like squeezing the toothpaste. There's no putting it back in the tube.

I have often told my children, "If you put something online, it's public and forever." Yet when I sent my e-mail, I believed no one else would see it other than the person I wrote—especially not the person I may have written *about*.

Who was I kidding?

I cannot control what happens to my words once they leave my cyberspace docking point. So I'd better be sure that I don't mind the content going viral, as they say.

Did my comments belittle someone? Were they derogatory, insulting, offensive? Did I speak as though in confidence about a private matter? Would I mind if the general public read what I wrote?

Jesus saw this coming. He warned that our whispered words would resound from the housetops (Luke 12:3). Was He thinking of e-mail, cell phones, Twitter, Instagram, Tik Tok, and all the humming avenues of social media that encircle our planet today?

"Let your speech always be with grace," Paul told first-century Christians, "seasoned with salt, that you may know how you ought to answer each one."

We all know salt is a preservative as well as a critical food seasoning. It keeps things from rotting or spoiling, and helps some items last longer. But I get the impression that Colossians 4:6 is talking about taste.

Overdo the salt, and the item is inedible.

When using salt on food, a little goes a long way. Consider salted caramels. Mmm, yes. Especially if that combination is anywhere near chocolate candy or lattes.

Seasoned with salt?

When my words hit the proverbial grapevine, I hope they taste like grace.

Oh Lord, Creator of all good things, help me make my words palatable, not punitive. Season them with Your goodness and grace. Amen.

> "Let the words of my mouth
> and the meditation of my heart
> be acceptable in Your sight,
> O Lord, my strength and my redeemer."
> Psalm 19:14

DAY TWENTY-FIVE

INTENTIONAL NEGLECT

"For God has not given us a spirit of fear,
but of power and of love and of a sound mind."
2 Timothy 1:7

If you google "intentional neglect" you'll find an array of complex information and discouraging news. It's not light reading.

However, that phrase lodged in my mind when our *pastor encouraged his Sunday-evening congregation to intentionally neglect those things that keep them from their goals and purposes.

He was not talking about neglecting people or responsibilities, but activities that grab hold of our attention and devour our time. Email. Television. Computer games. And other misplaced priorities that aren't necessarily bad.

He shared the story of a violinist who felt compelled to complete all her household chores before practicing. Her compulsion to clean took precedence over development of her gift. She finally realized that she would never become a virtuoso until she put her gift first.

Though I am not a violinist, I can relate with this woman's compulsive behavior for tying up loose ends. As I work at my writing, stealing hours and minutes throughout a busy day, I am constantly tempted by uncompleted chores around me—things that should be done.

The *shoulds* are deadly.

In personal application, intentional neglect means that I do only one household chore per day when I am under deadline, check only important email, and click off the internet before I'm tempted to read the latest headline, gossip, or gadget report.

Our pastor biblically encouraged us through Nehemiah 6, a chapter which outlines the distractions Nehemiah faced when trying to rebuild the wall of Jerusalem in the 400s BC. He had many detractors, yet he maintained his focus. How?

He prayed. He asked God to strengthen him.

Nehemiah's constant contact with the Lord kept him on target. He knew he was called, he knew his purpose, and he knew the source of his strength.

We have this same access to the God of creation, repair, and redemption. Do we go to Him for help?

We all neglect something because it is impossible to do everything. The question is, are we neglecting the right things?

Oh Lord, help me keep Your purposes in mind and stay with the task You have set before me. Be my strength and remind me that stewardship is important in my home, but compulsive adherence to self-imposed demands is not. Amen.

"Now therefore, O God, strengthen my hands."
Nehemiah 6:9

*Thank you, Pastor Brian Withrow

Day Twenty-Six

This Little Light

> "For You will light my lamp;
> the LORD my God will enlighten my darkness."
> Psalm 18:28

The television commercial darkened to a mountainous road, and a sleek new automobile sliced through the night, pulled like a toy car on a short string of light. As a faceless voice touted the manufacturer, camera angles tightened to a close-up viewpoint from behind the wheel, behind the headlights. The driver sped through the darkness on a mere two hundred feet of light, apparently unconcerned about what may lie beyond the beam or to either side.

Now that's faith.

As I watched the tiny silver car threading the darkness, I thought it was possibly the best illustration of faith I'd ever seen. God unquestionably calls us to walk by faith, to trust Him, to not wait for our vision to focus into His supreme eyesight, but to step out, following Him one step at a time within the boundary of the light He gives.

Two to three hundred feet of light sounds like too short of a lead for traveling through the darkness. But it is enough if the driver is not recklessly speeding.

Most often in my life I don't see the big picture—just the next step. I have to accept the fact that God can see much farther ahead than I. In fact, He sees the situation from beginning to end.

I remember a particularly difficult time during my husband's illness that I found comfort in a song on Christian radio. Its encouragement was to trust God, and do the next thing. Sometimes the next thing was simply making the bed, or doing the dishes, or shopping for groceries. I sensed that God knew I was surviving only one step at a time, with just enough faith to trust Him for the next one.

Psalm 119 hints at the limited lighting we're given, for it says God's Word is a lamp to our feet and a light to our path. That's pretty point specific, not all encompassing. I don't get to see the canyon yawning ahead, just the path I'm maneuvering at the moment.

This is no doubt the best way, for if I peered into the gorge, I might not notice the narrow path leading down the craggy sides, the hidden ways lying in secret crevices, or the bridge He has prepared to carry me safely across.

Oh, Lord, thank You for speaking to me in something as common and forgettable as my headlights. Help me remember every time I turn them on that You are giving me just the light I need to press through the darkness. Thank You, God, for Your faithfulness. Amen.

"The light shines in the darkness,
but the darkness has not overcome it."
John 1:5 NIV

Day Twenty-Seven

Space Beetle

"Likewise the Spirit also helps in our weaknesses.
For we do not know what we should pray for
as we ought,
but the Spirit Himself makes intercession for us."
Romans 8:26

Brea slipped out of her chair at the restaurant table and walked around to where I sat on the other side. At age three, she was a quiet little thing with big blue eyes and wispy brown hair. She squeezed between the chairs, climbed ever so carefully into my lap, and looked up at me through those sky-blue pools.

The noise of other diners in the crowded room vied with Brea's little voice. She was trying to tell me something, so I leaned closer to hear what she was saying.

"We saw the space beetle, Grandma."

"You did?"

"Yeah. It was big."

Space Beetle. I knew exactly what Brea meant. Our oldest son and his family had recently returned from a vacation in Seattle. Because of my own experiences and the knowledge of their trip, I could translate Brea's speech and understand her perfectly. She didn't have to use just the right words with me, and I did not say, "You mean the Space Needle?"

Just like God and me, I thought. *I don't always use the right words with Him, but neither do I recall Him ever telling me I said it wrong.*

Israel's great singer of songs said, "He has inclined His ear to me" (Psalm 116:2). Today we might say, "He leaned down to hear my small voice and listened to what I was saying."

Sometimes when life gets hard, I just crawl up in God's lap and cry, "I hurt. Hold me." Or "Lord, why?" Or simply, "Thank you." Because of His infinite knowledge and wisdom, He knows exactly what I mean. He even hears the cry of my heart when I can say nothing at all.

While Brea's little brother Braydn commanded his mother's attention at the end of the table, Brea whispered into my ear again, "I can sing a song, Grandma."

"Really? Will you sing it for me?"

"Twinkle, twinkle, little star, how I wonder what you are." The time-worn tune never sounded prettier.

God knows all the songs I sing too, but I think He likes to hear me sing them anyway.

Thank You, Lord, for letting me know You delight in my praises, that it pleases You when I seek Your presence. Thank You for letting me crawl up in Your lap and share my heart. Amen.

"I waited patiently for the LORD;
and He inclined to me."
Psalm 40:1

Day Twenty-Eight

Appearances Can Be Deceiving

> "Do not judge according to appearance,
> but judge with righteous judgment."
> John 7:24

Granite boulders litter the hillsides around our home. Some jut from the ridges like massive ships pushing free of earthen waves. Others lay strewn in crevices as though tossed by a playful hand. But nearly all of them bear patches of moss on their northern edges.

In the dry, parched months of summer, the moss clings to the rocks like brown, brittle scabs. But autumn rains revive the crusty layer to a deep velvety green. All winter and through the spring, it grows rich and thick, soft to the touch.

Each year I am surprised by the renewal of the moss. Ugly and lifeless during the summer, it is hard to believe that it could regenerate. But life is in it, and though dormant for a time, it resurrects each year.

There are people in my life who live their lives like the moss on granite boulders. How disappointed I am when I see family or close friends lying dormant in faith, appearing to give up on God in the middle of a dry spell or hard time. But the Lord reminds me of the danger in judging other hearts by what I see on the outside. I too have survived periods of dormancy, times in my spiritual life when I had little to show for my faith and beliefs. God has never written me off nor given up on me, for it is His life that lives within me, keeping me going through even the dormant times.

Thank You, Lord, that my life is in You, and that You don't give up on me. Thank You for regenerating my dry, parched spirit. Help me not to write off those around me who may be struggling, but to encourage them in Your faithfulness. Amen.

> "I have been crucified with Christ;
> it is no longer I who live, but Christ lives in me;
> and the life which I now live in the flesh
> I live by faith in the Son of God,
> who loved me and gave Himself for me."
> Galatians 2:20

Day Twenty-Nine

Cutting Back

"I am the true vine, and My Father is the vinedresser.
Every branch in Me that does not bear fruit
He takes away;
and every branch that bears fruit He prunes,
that it may bear more fruit."
John 15:1–2

Pruning my rose bushes is a painful process. It's not the thorny branches that cause me discomfort, but the emotional pain of cutting off green leaves and fragrant blooms. I feel like a butcher, hacking off limbs and twigs—an act I trust will condense the lifeblood of the plant and force it out again in bigger, better flowers.

The wisdom in this apparent paradox can be seen each year across California's San Joaquin Valley as orange growers brutally "box" their trees, shaving off the tops and sides. Peach trees sport flat-tops where farmers buzz their orchards like military recruits. Yet each spring, fragrant blossoms burst from their branches, promising rich fruit in the months to come.

Jesus used the illustration of pruning grapes to explain that God cares for His children in the same wise way a farmer tends his vineyard. He said His Father is the vine keeper who prunes back every fruit-bearing branch so it will bear more fruit.

I know God prunes me too—I can feel it. He cuts away the dead, unproductive habits in my life and trims back the good ones. It hurts when some desired outcome is delayed, or denied completely, and it's often hard to see God's love in a situation where I feel only disappointment.

It takes time—and trust—to see that when God cuts away errant growth, something more beautiful will appear in its place. Like the roses in my garden.

Lord, thank You for speaking to me through Your creation, reinforcing the truths of Your Word through my own garden. Help me remember that when I feel the pain of Your pruning, I can count on Your life-giving spirit to surge through me, producing bigger and better spiritual fruit for You. Amen.

> "But the fruit of the spirit is love, joy, peace, longsuffering, kindness, goodness, faithfulness, gentleness, self-control."
> Galatians 5:22–23

Day Thirty

In a Fog

"For we walk by faith, not by sight."
2 Corinthians 5:7

It was foggy. Very foggy. Again.

I didn't know which was worse: driving through blinding Colorado blizzards or navigating the thick pea-soup fog of central California. Either way, the front edge of my car's hood was as far as I could see.

Breathing a quick prayer for protection and X-ray vision, I headed down my driveway, onto the paved road and into near-zero visibility.

"Oh, God, thank You for the white line down the edge of the road that tells me how far I can go. Thank You for the yellow line in the center that shows me the danger zone and helps me stay on the right side."

Driving in the fog is so much like my life at times. Uncertainties bunch up around me like white cotton gauze, limiting my view of the future, choking my hope. I inch along disoriented by doubt, afraid to go too slowly for fear of being rear-ended by another clumsy Christian. Afraid to go too fast for fear of missing a bend in the road. My hungry eyes search for familiar landmarks, flags of faith that assure me I'll make it, and lights along the way that let me know I'm headed in the right direction.

But God didn't plan for me to venture out alone in a spiritual fog. He has given me direction and boundaries—faithfully painted lines on the road that whisper, "Don't pass here." Like a highway sign, His Word warns of curves ahead or dangerous crossings. He shows me the safe place within His limits.

"Slow down, gossip ahead," He says. "Don't drift off into envy of others who have nicer homes/cars/jobs than you. Watch out for potholes of greed or lust. Yield. Forgive."

When I can't see, He says, "Walk by faith." When I can't hear, He says, "I know your thoughts before you think them." And when I'm afraid, He says, "I am with you."

Thank God I don't have to wander through life alone, defenseless, or blind. Whether it be the fiercest emotional storm or thickest circumstantial haze, He is with me in every situation.

Lord, help me become so familiar with Your road signs that I can identify them even in the haze of doubt. Thank You for leading me through the fog. Amen.

> "Now faith is the substance of things hoped for, the evidence of things not seen."
> Hebrews 11:1

Day Thirty-One

Am I a Name Dropper?

"A good name is to be chosen
rather than great riches;
Loving favor rather than silver and gold."
Proverbs 22:1

My friend Jill is a name dropper. She raises Nigerian dwarf goats on her Kentucky farm, Sinai Thunder, and she drops a blessing on each animal born there.

As animal breeders do, she gives each kid a name that refers back to the dam and sire. But she also makes sure each name is a blessing that points to God.

A few examples of her goat names are: Sinai Thunder Chariots of Fire, called Cherry; Sinai Thunder Breath of Heaven, called Heaven; Sinai Thunder Miracle of Grace, called Gracie; and Sinai Thunder AD Luke, called Lukie.

She also has Redemption, Charity, Queen of Sheba, a buck named Agnus Dei, and a truckload of others. Did I mention she has more than one hundred goats?

But when she buys a goat from another breeder, its original name comes with it. If it's an uncomfortably negative moniker, she drops off the unlovely tag in her day-to-day handling of the animal and drops on a new name.

One doe's original name was Voodoo Princess. This pretty mama is now called Queenie—an upgrade in status as well as a blessing.

After considering the way Jill blesses her kids with godly names, I realized that God did this with His kids too. He dropped names all the time.

Remember Jacob who was renamed Israel? How about Abram and Sarai who became Abraham and Sarah?

In the New Testament Saul became Paul and Simon became Peter.

Name-dropping changed these people's lives and probably also changed the way others regarded them.

So I wonder, what names should I be dropping from and into my vocabulary? Have I tagged people with curses rather than blessings?

What do I call the children I'm around? Little Monster? Trouble-maker? Do I really want a child to carry those labels, or worse yet, live up to them?

I plan to do some name-dropping—getting rid of old nicknames and coming up with new ones. How about you? Let's drop a few blessings on those we come in contact with and see what a difference it makes.

Oh Lord, help me think before I use a derogatory name for someone, particularly a child – even in my thoughts. And may I bless them instead with a name of hope and encouragement. Amen.

"Fear not, for I have redeemed you;
I have called you by your name; you are Mine!"
Isaiah 43:1

Day Thirty-Two

Boundaries: When Enough Is More Than Enough

"But the wise answered, saying,
'No, lest there should not be enough for us and you;
but go rather to those who sell,
and buy for yourselves.'"
Matthew 25:9

"I'm exhausted," a fellow teacher said, collapsing into a chair in my classroom. She was considering cutting back on some of her activities.

"You can't do everything," I offered. In no way was I preaching to her. I was simply repeating my own personal mantra: I can't do it all.

It's hard for me to say no to a worthy cause. My friend had the same problem. There are so many worthwhile activities that need our participation, not to mention all the work required to keep our homes and jobs up and running.

I once read a wonderful little booklet titled *Tyranny of the Urgent,* by Charles E. Hummel. Through it I learned that urgent tasks scream at us to be completed, but they are things we wouldn't mind having someone else do. Like yard work or house cleaning.

Important things are those that I would not let someone else do: reading bedtime stories, making brownies for a family picnic, or caring for a sick loved one. The urgent can usually wait; the truly important cannot.

But how do I choose from all those important things outside my home that vie for my limited time?

Jesus told the parable of ten young women who waited all night for a traditional wedding celebration to begin. Five were prepared with extra oil for their lamps, and five were not. When the call rang out at midnight, the five without enough oil asked the others to share. They did not.

The point of the parable was to be prepared. But I believe the Lord was also trying to show us something about personal boundaries. Sometimes we have to say no rather than use up everything we have—like our energy, time, and emotional strength.

Will the world come to a premature end if I don't attend that workshop? Do I really need to serve on another committee? Will anyone care if my floor isn't mopped today?

Life without limits—or boundaries—can be dangerous. We can't do everything, but we can pray about the requests for our time and ask God what His priorities are. Once we know, we decline everything else—graciously.

And finally, we must not let guilt rob us of our rest. An afternoon with "nothing" to do is an opportunity to recharge, go for a walk, or thank the Lord for leading us in our decisions.

Oh God of endless energy, thank You for the blessing of boundaries, and for helping me prioritize according to Your will. Amen.

> "Lord, You alone are my portion and my cup; …
> The boundary lines have fallen for me
> in pleasant places."
> Psalm 16:5–6 NIV

DAY THIRTY-THREE

GIVE AND LIVE

"It is more blessed to give than to receive."
Acts 20:35

Most of the sixth graders to whom I taught ancient world history thought it would be cool to float on the salty waters of Israel's Dead Sea.

Ancient Israel was part of the California educational standards for Social Studies. On the map, ancient and otherwise, the Dead Sea is the giant dot at the bottom of the Jordan River's lengthy exclamation point. But the high salinity (34 percent) that enables people to float in the Dead Sea is what prevents marine life from existing there. No fish, no worms, no plant life other than a bit of seasonal algae. It is indeed a dead sea.

The Jordan River flows south from its mountainous source into the Sea of Galilee, down the Jordan Valley, and empties at last into a seemingly bottomless pit of salt-heavy water. The sea lies fifteen hundred feet below sea level, and more than fifty-five inches of water evaporate from it in a year's time due to the intense, dry heat of the valley.

According to the Dead Sea tourism guide, its water contains twenty-one minerals, twelve of which are found in no other sea or ocean. The Dead Sea contains ten times more salt and minerals than the Mediterranean Sea and draws people to its water for therapeutic reasons.

But the Dead Sea has no outlet. Nothing flows out of its abundant, mineral-laced reserve. A selfish sea, it is always taking in, never giving out. This too is what makes it dead.

It's not hard to be like the Dead Sea—stingy, hoarding, unsharing—always taking and never giving. Usually, when I feel unproductive or stale, it's because I'm bogged down in myself. I'm not listening to or praying for others, not giving my time or sharing toward their need.

When my vision turns inward, that's when I become like the Dead Sea—a bottomless, lifeless pool. I need to kick out the crusty, dried banks of stinginess and pour into others the blessing-filled waters of God's unreserved love.

Lord, help me let Your living water flow through me to others. Help me not to clog the lines with greed, keeping it all for myself. Show me how I can give—and live. Amen.

"He who believes in Me as the Scripture has said, out of his heart will flow rivers of living water."
John 7:38

Day Thirty-Four

What Goes Here?

> "As each one has received a gift,
> minister it to one another,
> as good stewards of the manifold grace of God."
> 1 Peter 4:10

*I*t was the last week of Christmas vacation, and I had planned to spend all day Wednesday in my classroom cleaning up leftover decorations, writing lesson plans, and getting ready for the next week of school. It was going to be a nice, leisurely day with no interruptions, no schedules, and no students. The anticipation of being well prepared was heady.

When I unlocked the door to my classroom at a quarter to seven that morning and turned on the light, that anticipation soured like week-old banana bread. Papers were spread across tables and countertops, a half-empty paper cup sat on my desk, and my radio station had been changed. Administrators were using my room to teach a winter intervention class, and they didn't tell me! I was not happy.

I felt put upon, abused, and unfairly uninformed. What about my plans? How dare they upset my plans?

The other teacher was surprised to see me at the desk when she came in an hour later. She assured me that class would be over by 11:55 a.m. and invited me to stay and work while she and her fourth graders finished their assignments. Shamed by the fact that I could get so angry so fast when I really wanted to be more like Jesus, I gathered my lesson plans and ungraded papers from before Christmas and, as cheerfully as possible, told her I'd be back Friday afternoon.

That teacher didn't ask to be put in room twelve so she could interfere with my plans. And whose room was it, anyway? Not mine; I just worked there. The room belonged to the school, and the district let me—and paid me—to teach there.

How much more joyful my life would be if I spent less time complaining and more time discovering *God's* plans.

Forgive me, Lord, for my self-righteous indignation. Help me remember I'm a servant, a steward, working for You. Help me remember that I'm not really in control of anything except my attitude. Amen.

> "Well done, good and faithful servant;
> you were faithful over a few things,
> I will make you ruler over many things.
> Enter into the joy of your lord."
> Matthew 25:21

DAY THIRTY-FIVE

GLORY

"The glory of young men is their strength,
and the splendor of old men is their gray head."
Proverbs 20:29

Cream-colored eye shadow followed by dark brown eyeliner and black mascara—my early morning makeup ritual was right on schedule when I saw the stray eyelash lying softly against my face, just to the right of my eye. Gently, I flicked at it, careful not to stretch the tender eye area skin, only to discover that it wouldn't flick.

It wasn't an eyelash. It was a wrinkle.

I knew it hadn't been there the day before because I put on my makeup then too and I had not seen it. I flicked again. No good. It lay there, tucked into my skin with perky permanence.

Age is something I tend to forget until I put on my makeup or try pulling on my jeans one leg at a time while standing. It hurts now. It didn't used to. I'm fighting against sitting down to get dressed—I'm not ready to be old.

My mother once said in her later years that she didn't know how to act because she had never been that old before. It made me laugh at the time, but I think it was her way of fighting against the inevitable. She never gave up and died in her sleep because she didn't see it coming.

I've always tried to distinguish between growing older and growing old. To me, growing older means gaining wisdom, experience, graciousness. Growing older means shedding the shackles of caring about what other people think and not being afraid to try something new. Babies grow older. So do redwood trees and teenagers (thank God). But growing old is what bread does: it just sits there and molds.

God tells me that gray hair can be a crown of glory when accompanied by righteous living (Proverbs 16:31). I have plenty of gray hair. It started turning in my twenties. I prefer to call it silver, but rarely do I feel glorious. Could it be that I'm just sitting around sprouting mold instead of continuing to grow spiritually?

My strength may be waning, but my prayer life shouldn't be. My eyesight may be weakening, but my spiritual vision should be sharper. My hearing may be diminishing, but do I recognize the voice of God more clearly than I did in my youth?

I want to spend the rest of my life telling my children and others of God's faithfulness and declaring with the psalmist, "O God, You have taught me from my youth, and to this day I declare Your wondrous works" (Psalm 71:17).

How good it is to grow older in the Lord, closer to Him, stronger in Him. What splendor there is in experiencing the faithfulness of His ways and realizing that most of the things I worried about never happened.

Lord, as I step closer each hour of my life to the moment of stepping into Your presence, help me remember that I'm still growing in You. Amen.

"Now also when I am old and gray-headed, O God,
do not forsake me,
until I declare Your strength to this generation."
Psalm 71:18

Day Thirty-Six

A Thousand Hills

"For every beast of the forest is Mine,
and the cattle on a thousand hills."
Psalm 50:10

Our home overlooks rolling ridges of oak-dotted hills, heaped up like green blankets at the foot of God's bed. Cattle, coyotes, and other creatures roam this land, and the trees and brooks ring with bird song. It's as though we live in the "thousand hills"—that biblical land where all the beasts and birds belong to God.

I often watch the cattle grazing, drowsily munching their way up the hills. No clocks tick out their pace, no schedules dictate their wandering. They simply graze, confident of the next mouthful.

During those times when money is short and time is tight, I look at those cows and think, *Can't we have just one of those symbolic cows, Lord? They are all there—all the cattle on these hills that figuratively represent Your provision. You know our need and my impatience; why is it taking so long?*

The psalm that tells me about the thousand hills also tells me what God wants: "Offer to God thanksgiving and pay your vows to the Most High. Call upon Me in the day of trouble; I will deliver you, and you shall glorify Me" (Psalm 50:14–15).

I think He wants me to trust Him as confidently as those cows trust the hill to provide their next bite. Do I trust Him with all my heart? Will I praise Him even while waiting for His answer to my request?

It is so hard for me to be patient. I guess that's what makes it a sacrifice.

Thank You, Lord, for being patient with me when I'm not very good at being patient with You. Thank You for loving me anyway and for providing for my family. Amen.

> "Dwell in the land and feed on His faithfulness."
> Psalm 37:3

Day Thirty-Seven

Listen

"Go out and stand on the mountain
before the Lord."
1 Kings 19:11

Everyone in my family goes to the gym to work out except me. I'm just not into the group exercise trend, and I keep insisting that I don't have time to drive back and forth to town just to get sweaty.

So I walk.

I walk down and back up the half-mile road that winds up the hill to our home. When I first began the regimen, I had to stop repeatedly on the upward trek just to catch my breath. Now I stop to listen.

Just before sunset, horned owls waken from their daytime naps, hooting throaty love songs across the ravines. Cows call their calves, frogs croon near the pond, ducks flutter and quack. Unless I stand completely still, I miss much of the evening's symphony.

The brush of my jeans, leg against leg, and the crunch of gravel beneath my tennis shoes are loud enough to flush out a covey of quail, annoy the ducks, and startle a red-tailed hawk from its treetop roost. But when I stop and listen, I hear the chirps and songs of small birds, the hum of crickets, and a breath of wind in the tall grass. I invariably hear *peace*.

Too much of my life is spent in a rush, hurrying from one appointment to another, trying to cram too many activities into one day's time. How rarely do I just stop...and listen? Television and traffic, phones and family all vie for my attention. It becomes harder and harder to find a quiet time, still myself, and listen to God.

When Elijah sought out the Lord, God told him to go stand on the mountain. Wind crashed into the rocky cliffs, crushing them like candy. An earthquake shook the ground and fire swept the scene, but Elijah heard God speak to him in a quiet, hushed voice. To hear that voice, Elijah had to be quiet himself.

I don't want to be so busy that I fly through life doing all the talking, making all the noise, and missing out on the peace of God around me.

Lord, help me take the time to stop and listen. Thank You for not shouting, for not getting lost in the clamor. Thank You that I have to quiet myself to hear Your still, small voice. Amen.

> "Be still, and know that I am God."
> Psalm 46:10

Day Thirty-Eight

My Mother's Keeper

"Can a woman forget her nursing child,
and not have compassion on the son of her womb?"
Isaiah 49:15

I checked to see that she was dry, not hungry. Her bedding comfortable and clean, her clothes warm. I smiled and told her quietly about my day as I smoothed her hair and kissed her cheek.

Mother—she had become my child. I prayed for her, the one who taught me to pray. I spoke of Jesus to the one who first spoke His name to me. I was the mother now, comforting, encouraging, making the hard decisions to sell her house, store her things, and tell her she couldn't drive anymore.

"I haven't seen him yet today," she said softly.

"Who?" I asked, wondering if this time it was Dad—long since gone—or Jesus, whom she said she had seen once before.

Several minutes passed as thoughts washed over her face and tried to form on her lips. "I want to call him Fredrick."

"What did he do?" I asked. The question hung in the air like a sock on a clothesline.

"I think he stole my heart," she said as though a young girl again, closing her eyes.

I had not heard of Fredrick before. As far as I knew, there were no Fredricks in our family line. An old boyfriend, perhaps, brought back to her stroke-riddled memory with other bits of the past, none of the present, not even me.

"I'm going to leave now, Mother, and let you rest," I said after a few moments.

Stirring, she opened her eyes. "I'm not tired. I'm just busy with my dreams."

"That's good," I said. "Always hold on to your dreams."

My mother was dying and I told her to hold on to her dreams. Was I crazy? Should I have said something else? Though why shouldn't she hold on to her dreams after all these years? Sarah had and conceived Isaac, the promised son.

Maybe Mother dreamed of independence, living again in her own home, walking outside by herself, going out with friends. All those dreams would soon come true for her when she stepped into heaven's light.

In those final days of not knowing where she was or why Dad wasn't with her, Mother still knew Jesus. She had not lost her knowledge of Him, as many elderly do in the grip of Alzheimer's or dementia. She knew He loved her, saved her, and was waiting for her. She knew Him when she didn't know me. And that was enough.

Thank You, Lord, for always being there for Mother. Be so present in my life that when all else fades away, I will still know that You are there for me. Amen.

> "Even to your old age, I am He.
> And even to gray hairs I will carry you!"
> Isaiah 46:4

Day Thirty-Nine

Dominion

> "Let Us make man in Our image,
> according to Our likeness;
> let them have dominion over the fish of the sea,
> over the birds of the air,
> and over the cattle, over all the earth
> and over every creeping thing
> that creeps on the earth."
> Genesis 1:26

Oh Lord, she thinks Dad is still alive and living in the basement.

Prayers like this were common for me since Mother's stroke. She didn't have Alzheimer's disease, but multiple small strokes had short-circuited parts of her memory and reasoning. Dad had been gone for seven years, and there was no basement in the lovely assisted-living home where she stayed. To make matters worse, her dog was dying.

I'd prayed that Meagan—the half-breed Husky—would die a natural death, but it clung tenaciously to its deaf, blind, and arthritic existence. By my calculations, the dog had to be near twenty, and the owners of Mother's residence had graciously allowed us to bring it there to live in the backyard. At first, Mother saw Meagan daily, and both woman and dog would rally for a few moments in each other's familiar company.

Soon the dog's bad teeth prevented it from eating and it didn't even have the strength to scratch away the fleas. Mother's caregivers begged me to put the dog down, out of its misery. "We can't stand to see it suffer," they would say when I visited. They told me Meagan wouldn't move from a favorite spot by the back porch when it rained, but would lie in the water as it filled the depression.

God, I can't do this! I wouldn't do this to Mother, and her condition is nearly as bad. How can I do this to her dog? Mother has trouble eating, too, and some days she doesn't even know me! How can I take away the only thing she seems to recognize?

Over the next few days I wrestled with the decision. Which would be better: to let the dog live and possibly drown in its sleep, or ask the veterinarian to force its sleep and put an end to the suffering? I was quite adept at rallying to either side of the issue until the Holy Spirit brought Genesis 1:26 to mind.

God said He gave us dominion over the animals. That means He gave us the authority and the right to make decisions about them—to control them, to rule them. He didn't give us dominion over people, so there was no danger of misinterpreting the merciful ending of a dog's suffering life with the euthanasia practiced among the sick and elderly in some places. My decision was clear.

The morning I picked up Meagan, I found the dog lying in its hole. It didn't hear me yell its name, and turned startled, cataract-covered eyes to me when I gently touched it. The old bones seemed held together only by loose skin, and I carried it to the car with tears in my eyes. The veterinarian's receptionist recognized my mission, and taking Meagan's leash, she assured me that everything would be all right.

I didn't have to tell Mother about Meagan the next time I visited her. With all the many things she didn't know, remember, or recognize, she seemed to know that Meagan was gone, and it was okay. She understood—even when she didn't believe me when I told her Dad wasn't living in the basement.

O God, thank You for helping me through that valley of decision that was so hard for me. Thank You for showing me that taking responsibility sometimes means doing the hard, disagreeable thing. Thank You for Your mercy, and for caring even about our animals. Amen.

> "A righteous man regards the life of his animal,
> But the tender mercies of the wicked are cruel."
> Proverbs 12:10

Day Forty

Small Talk

> "Let your speech always be with grace,
> seasoned with salt,
> that you may know how you ought to
> answer each one."
> Colossians 4:6

Cam was the owner of a very busy auto-repair shop. He went to our church and our cars went to his shop. While he and I waited for one of his employees to finish with my car, we made small talk.

He bent beneath the yawning hood of an ailing vehicle and looked for the mechanical culprit. "How's teaching?" he asked.

I told him teaching was great, but I was thinking of applying to another school district. The school I had in mind was difficult to get into. Not a lot of turnover among teachers there.

Voicing my frustration at not really having much control over the situation, I quipped, "I guess it's up to the Lord." It was a standard Christian response among many believers, a nice godly thing to say at almost any juncture. But the words had barely slipped from my mouth when I realized their weight.

Cam closed his eyes and reached farther into the car's engine. "It all is," he said quietly. "It all is."

I had tossed out the platitude without thinking. This man had buried his twenty-seven-year-old daughter a few weeks earlier and I was complaining about something as trivial as where I wanted to work.

Cam's daughter died in an automobile accident, and practically the entire town attended the funeral, as well as the police chief, the fire marshal, and city officials. Not only was Cam a healer of auto ailments, he was also a city councilman and a leader in the church. Everyone knew Cam, and his daughter's funeral had been a testimony of faith in the face of tragedy. A testimony of how to keep praising God when bad things happen to good people.

I saw in the closing of his eyes his quiet acceptance of my casual statement and the cost of what it meant to really believe it. Though I had carelessly tossed the words into the conversation, he knew how true they really were.

The silence stretched. I wondered if I should apologize for my thoughtlessness. Reluctant to open the wound any further I said, "I guess the only thing we can control is our response."

Cam backed out from under the hood. Ever gracious, he laughed and nodded, picking up on my attempt to lighten the moment. "And hopefully a couple of automobile engines every now and then."

Too many times I speak without thinking. Maybe I'm just trying to be friendly or maybe I'm just trying to fill dead air. I have wasted many idle words, and the Lord reminds me to carefully consider what I say to people. He tells me to season my words with grace, to choose those that heal or encourage, warn or instruct. There really is no such thing as small talk. It all carries more weight than we might think.

Oh God, help me to be more thoughtful of those to whom I speak and not waste an opportunity to build them up or point them to You. Amen.

> "Let no corrupt communication proceed
> out of your mouth,
> but what is good for necessary edification,
> that it may impart grace to the hearers."
> Ephesians 4:29

Day Forty-One

Scarred But Standing

"Behold, I make all things new."
Revelation 21:5

"I didn't see that one coming!"

"How could God let this happen?"

"What now?"

Have you ever uttered one of the above comments after a startling or tragic event? I dare say, most have. We lose our job, our home, our love, our way. We struggle to get back up, dig out the gravel pitting our flesh, and continue on.

But we're never quite the same.

A note on my desktop computer's screen says: "Battles result in scars. No one gets out unscathed." It serves to remind me that the characters in my books will be wounded.

Scars remind us of painful experiences, even of lessons learned. Such reminders often strengthen us. However, those scars are not *who* we are.

"You're not defined by your injuries," says the heroine in one of my books. She is appalled that her neighbor sees himself only through his life-changing wounds from a tour of duty in Afghanistan.

"We're all crippled and short-sighted in some way," she insists. "Physically or spiritually or mentally."

Both the main characters in the story bear gaping wounds—one physical, the other emotional. And both must decide if they trust God enough to let Him reach into those wounds and heal them—to "make all things new."

Christ gave us a second chance at Calvary but it didn't stop there. He continues to renew us by His Spirit every single day. And His Word refreshes us and gives us courage to get back up and keep going in spite of our handicaps.

It's hard.

We may look different.

But battle scars and wounds are simply that— scars and wounds. Beautiful treasures beneath the scarred hand of our resurrected Healer.

God is the great recycler of human wreckage, but we must allow His touch.

Oh Lord, You know what it means to be wounded and scarred. Thank You for taking on such things for our sake. Amen.

> "From now on let no one trouble me,
> for I bear in my body the marks of the Lord Jesus."
> Galatians 6:17

Day Forty-Two

Storing the Light

"The light shines in the darkness,
and the darkness has not overcome it."
John 1:5 NIV

*W*e recently installed a solar porch light at the back of the house. On sunny days, it stores enough light to cast a moon-like glow beneath the pergola at night, lighting a pathway to our back door.

Solar garden lights also mark the entry to our driveway, intended to keep people from turning into the ditch or driving over the railroad ties on either side.

I enjoy not only the ambiance of the solar-powered lights but their no-care convenience as well. I can count on the little illuminators to do their job unhindered. Unless, of course, the weather interferes.

If a day is overcast or snowy, the solar cells collect nothing and remain dark the following night.

They're just like me.

When I let the busyness of my life get the upper hand, I may not meet with the Lord in the morning. Too many mornings like that, and I'm not collecting the wisdom, hope, or comfort of God that I glean from reading His Word and spending time in prayer.

Darkness—the absence of light—can easily wash in around me, especially in the night of my struggles. Discouragement can gain a foothold, growing like silent mold in a dark place.

But even the smallest glow of light flickers against the blackest void. It cannot be hidden—it shines. And no matter how feeble it may be, it offers hope to those who are searching for a spark of life.

Remember the old cliché about seeing the light at the end of the tunnel? There's something to that. Just a pinpoint of light draws us out of the darkness.

It's Son Light I need—and the more I store up by spending time with the Lord and listening to what He has to say, the brighter my own light shines.

Lord, help me not to neglect charging my soul-cells with the light of Your Word and presence. Thank You for shining, even in my darkest hour. Amen.

> "I am the light of the world.
> He who follows Me shall not walk in darkness,
> but have the light of life."
> John 8:12

Day Forty-Three

Your Oxygen

> "The Spirit of God has made me,
> and the breath of the Almighty gives me life."
> Job 33:4

As the plane taxied out to the runway for my return flight home, I again heard the familiar emergency instructions from a flight attendant at the front of the cabin.

If the cabin lost pressure, an oxygen mask would release from the overhead compartment directly above each passenger. Using a demonstration mask, she showed us how to slip the elastic band over the back of our heads, secure the mask over nose and mouth, and breathe normally.

Then she cautioned that in the event of such an emergency, we were to put on our own mask before helping the person seated next to us—even if that person was a child.

The warning had a heartless ring to it, but it soon made sense. How could I help anyone else if I was about to lose consciousness myself?

This practical, life-saving advice applies to other areas of my life as well, yet too often I fail to consider its logic. Instead, I offer advice to friends in difficult situations when I don't have a solid grip on my own challenges. I try to give them answers when I'm not even certain of the questions.

It all comes down to preparation. Am I grounded in the Word of God? Do I know where my lifeline is—my emotional and spiritual oxygen mask—in case of depressurization?

Sadly, many of us don't. We don't spend time every day reading the promises and assurances of God. We don't fill ourselves with the confidence of His faithfulness. Therefore, when the air gets thin, we start to panic. What good will we be to anyone else in that condition, much less to ourselves?

Jesus said, "Love your neighbor as yourself" (Matthew 19:19). Do I really love myself the way God wants me to, or do I ignore His grace and belittle myself for not measuring up? Do I love myself enough to get the spiritual nourishment I need?

Lord, remind me that I need to stay connected to You for my spiritual life and wellbeing. Your Word allows me to take a deep breath of Your life-giving wisdom. Help me be prepared so I'll be able to help others near me who may be gasping for air. Amen.

> "And the LORD God formed man
> of the dust of the ground,
> and breathed into his nostrils the breath of life;
> and man became a living being."
> Genesis 2:7

Day Forty-Four

Can God Forget?

> "For I will forgive their iniquity,
> and their sin I will remember no more."
> Jeremiah 31:34

A recent social media meme commented on age by saying "the other day" could mean two days ago or fifteen years.

Funny, but sadly true. Forgetfulness seems to plague us the more we need to remember. But at least God doesn't forget things.

Or does He?

Yes, He does. By choice. His is not selective memory but rather, deliberate forgetfulness.

In Psalm 103:12 we read that God has removed our sins from us as far as the east is from the west. I'm sure glad He didn't choose a northerly or southerly direction instead.

As a teacher of ancient world history, I often used a globe in the classroom to demonstrate the cardinal directions of north, east, south, and west. A favorite activity was asking students to choose a starting point with their finger and move it around the globe heading east. Or west. Either would do.

If they moved in an easterly direction, I asked if they would run into west. If they were moving west, I asked if they would run into east.

I had them try the same thing starting at the top or north point of the globe, moving their finger down in a southerly route. Eventually, they hit "south" or the South Pole, but if they kept going, their direction changed and they were heading north, aimed at the North Pole.

The point was, south and north meet, even though the starting points are thousands of miles apart. They turn back on each other again and again *even though a traveler keeps moving straight ahead*. But east and west never meet.

I believe God deliberately chose east and west when He spoke of our sins being removed. The only way we can run into them again is if we turn around and go back to them.

Thank You, God, that because of Jesus' sacrifice, You have put our sins behind You and choose to forget them. And thank You that when You do, it's a done deal. Amen.

"You will cast all our sins into the depths of the sea."
Micah 7:19

Day Forty-Five

Mom-Care

> "As one whom his mother comforts,
> so I will comfort you."
> Isaiah 66:13

What is it about a mother that makes her do things for her children all the time? Even when no one's looking? Even when no one knows? Especially her children.

I believe it's the God-gene in her—not in a scientific, physiological sense, but in a spiritual sense. God's fingerprint is on His creation. He breathed the breath of life into Adam from whom He created a woman. Adam named her Eve because she was the mother of all living.

Of course it's a God thing.

Who else would go through pain for our deliverance?

Who else would give without thanks and then give again anyway?

Who else would say, "I'll take care of you," and then do it even when we're not looking?

There's a little crossover between Mom-care and God-care.

Psalm 121:7 tells me the Lord will keep me safe and watch over me, and He does it all the time, even when I don't know it.

When the auto-service technician called me out to my car the other day to see the split rubber on the inside of the left front tire, I remembered that verse.

The left front tire is the closest to oncoming traffic. All the other tires on my car were in good shape. There was an imbalance somewhere, a misalignment that I didn't know about. The fix was easy, but the damages could have been horrific.

This was not the first time the Lord had watched over my life, nor will it be the last.

I often see Mom-care in His protection, just as I saw God-care in the mother I remember.

"Love Jesus more than anyone, even me," she often said.

It was the best advice I've ever been given.

Thanks, Mom.

Thank You, Lord, for a mother who loved You and taught me about Your faithfulness. Help me teach it to my own children and to others with whom I come in contact. Amen.

> "The LORD shall preserve your going out
> and your coming in
> from this time forth,
> and even forevermore."
> Psalm 121:8

Day Forty-Six

Please, Bug Me

"Yet you do not have because you do not ask."
James 4:2

Some people don't want to be bothered. God is not one of them.

Jesus told His followers of a man who banged on his neighbor's door in the middle of the night because he needed extra food for an unexpected guest. The neighbor said, "Go away. It's late. Everyone's in bed. I'm not getting up."

But he did. He got up and gave the man what he needed.

Why?

Not because he liked the guy, but because the neighbor kept banging on the door.

Do we pray like that? Do we go to God and pound on the door until we get an answer? Jesus said we should. He told us to ask, seek, and knock.

Jesus didn't speak English, so I don't think He lined the words up like that so they'd spell out a neat little acrostic: Ask Seek Knock—ASK. I believe He was showing us three levels of communication and commitment.

When I worked as a reporter for a mid-size daily newspaper, I operated in these levels nearly every day.

"Is flagpole one word or two?" I could shoot out a question in the newsroom while sitting at my desk and hear someone throw back an answer. Asking required very little effort.

Seeking took a little more work. I had to stop what I was doing, pick up the *Associated Press Stylebook* and look up the answer. It meant searching, discovering, discerning.

Knocking involved total commitment. If I wanted to see the chief editor or general manager about something, I had to get out of my chair, go to his office, and knock on the door.

If he was busy, I had to come back and try again.

If he left for lunch when I wasn't looking, I had to go to him when he returned. Persisting was the only way I could talk to one of them face-to-face if I required direction, wanted to lodge a complaint, or needed to pick up an assignment. It took the most effort.

So, what kind of prayers do we pray? How much effort do we put into talking to God?

Yes, the Lord knows the very thoughts of our hearts, unlike the editor or general manager. But I believe Jesus gave us a bit of vital information when He said to ask, seek, and knock.

How badly do we want to hear from God?

Are we pounding on the door?

Thank You, Lord, for always hearing my prayer, and for always giving me the answer I need rather than just the answer I want. Thank You for Your great faithfulness. Amen.

> "For everyone who asks receives,
> and he who seeks finds,
> and to him who knocks it will be opened."
> Luke 11:10

DAY FORTY-SEVEN

POUR IT OUT

"Behold, to obey is better than sacrifice,
and to heed than the fat of rams."
1 Samuel 15:22

*T*he graceful lines of a beautiful pitcher draw me like a thirsty soul to a bubbling spring. Several styles in various colors top an antique hutch in my dining room.

Hand-thrown pottery is my favorite. Others are tin spatter-ware, ceramic or glass, and a few old tin coffee pots that join the array, often filled with fresh flowers.

Rare mugs sometimes squeeze into the line-up with their hearty handles and heavy weight. But mugs don't have the one qualifier that sets apart a decanter: the lip that pours out.

It appears I have a penchant for pitchers.

It began one Sunday years ago when our pastor asked us to write down the dreams of our heart—the things we really wanted to do. He handed out envelopes for us to fill with our dream, address to ourselves, and seal. He promised to mail them six months later.

My dream was to become a columnist and a novelist. As a long-time journalist and freelance writer, I was familiar with publishing. But as much as I wanted to be a newspaper columnist who wrote about her own ideas and not just the news, I was terrified that I'd run out of things to say. Then what would I do?

The Lord led me to the Old Testament story of the widow's oil in 2 Kings 4. Elisha told the needy woman to collect all the vessels she could find, take the little bit of oil she had left, and pour it into the vessels. When she ran out of containers, she was to sell enough of them to pay her debts and then live on the rest.

The widow didn't run out of oil as long as she was pouring. The flow didn't stop until she had filled all the containers she could gather. And that's where the Lord spoke to me about my writing:

"As long as you pour it out, I will pour it in."

Obedience and trust were key components for the widow, and they became as important to me as well. In the last several years I have written columns, blogs, novels, and devotionals for internationally known publishers. The Lord has faithfully "poured in" as I have poured out.

My pitchers remind me of His promise and His desire for obedience and trust.

What has the Lord said He would provide so you could in turn pour it out? Try Him. See if He is as good as His word. And decide if you will be a pitcher or a mug.

Thank You, God, for Your great faithfulness, and for giving me abundantly what I need in order to do what You have called me to do. Amen.

> "Trust in the Lord, and do good;
> Dwell in the land, and feed on His faithfulness."
> Psalm 37:3

Day Forty-Eight

Resting in His Shadow

"He who dwells in the secret place of the Most High shall abide under the shadow of the Almighty."
Psalm 91:1

American lyricist Oscar Hammerstein II said the hills were alive with the sound of music.

Where I once lived, that music played against spring-green hillsides. Black angus cattle dotted the scene like quarter notes on a musical score. In the spring, each cow had a calf at her side, and she paced her stride to match its own faltering steps.

The calves shone like onyx in the morning sun, dark and sleek against the grass their mothers grazed. There was a tenderness in it all—in the grass, in the animals, in the freshness of the mornings—a moment set against the rush of time when nothing mattered but the protection and nurturing of new life.

I drove through that landscape every weekday morning on my way to school. And in the late afternoons I returned on the same road to find long shadows thrown across the pastures by the grazing cattle.

One day the cows had turned their eyes away from the low sun, and their backs toward the west. I slowed to watch them, wondering what there was of God out in that pasture. I knew there was something—something He would show me of Himself if I paused in my hurry home and searched for His message.

The cow closest to the fence line along the road stood at an odd angle, sideways to the slanting sunlight. Her shadow stretched wide across the grass, and several feet away lay her resting calf, tucked exactly within the edges of her cool shade, sheltered from the heat of the day.

She knew.

She knew exactly how to stand to shade her calf, and she stayed there until the glare of the sun had passed.

Our God knows too. He knows we need respite from the heat of worry and stress. He also knows *when* we need it, and He is there to let us rest in the shadow of His presence.

And if we still our hearts and listen, we may hear the music of His love around us.

Oh God of all comfort, thank You for knowing us better than we know ourselves, and for giving us exactly what we need. Amen.

> "The LORD your God in your midst,
> the Mighty One, will save;
> He will rejoice over you with gladness,
> He will quiet you in His love,
> He will rejoice over you with singing."
> Zephaniah 3:17

DAY FORTY-NINE

SCRATCHING AT GOD-KNOWS-WHAT

"And my God shall supply all your need
according to His riches in glory by Christ Jesus."
Philippians 4:19

After moving back to Colorado, we lived for a year in an area referred to as "Hardscrabble." The name arrived with gold seekers and farmers scrabbling to make a living off a pebbly patch of Rocky Mountain soil. The scrabble even showed between the sparse blades of winter grass in our side yard, where sparrows pecked and scratched for God-knows-what.

They scraped the barren, wind-blown ground, and in answer to their tireless quest I hung a new cedar bird feeder, filled to the brim with wild-bird food and sunflower seeds.

They ignored it.

No birds alighted the following day either, but I assured myself that like the springtime hummingbirds homing in on their favorite nectar, so would the sparrows. *Give them a day*, I told myself. *They'll find it.*

On the third day, there were still no birds at the feeder. They scratched the bare earth, heads down, flushing away when the dog bounded round the corner and into their foraging grounds.

The fourth day, they were at it again, busily scraping with their frail little feet, heads bent to the bare ground, pecking now and again at an imaginary seed. I could almost hear their frantic thoughts: *There has to be something to eat in here somewhere!*

And all the time above them hung my feeder, still full to the brim of the choicest fowl fare.

I stood at the window watching, wondering if they would ever notice my care for them. I've had feeders at every home, and always the birds have found them and filled their gullets.

It wasn't hard to see that I was much like those Hardscrabble sparrows, bent on my own way of providing what I needed, unwilling to look up to another who waited close by, provision in hand. How often do I flit past my Bible, too busy to stop and feed on its life-giving words? How often do I pursue God-knows-what in my quest for sustenance?

And that is just the point: God knows what. He knows what I need and has provided it. Why do I so often seek my own way instead of His?

Thank You, Lord, for always having what I need. Forgive me for not coming to You first. Amen.

"Do not fear therefore;
you are of more value than many sparrows."
Matthew 10:31

Day Fifty

They've Come!

> "You prepare a table before me
> in the presence of my enemies;
> You anoint my head with oil; my cup runs over."
> Psalm 23:5

At last, the finches and sparrows had come to my feeder. It took a foot of snow, freezing temperatures, and chilling wind, but they came.

The feeder had been hanging outside my living room window for weeks while the birds skittered and scratched around beneath it, ignoring its luscious fare.

Finally, when they couldn't work things out on their own, couldn't find enough to eat, couldn't dig through twelve inches of snow with their twig-like legs, they looked up and there it was. Full and easily accessible.

This sounds so much like my personal journey with God.

Does He, in His infinite wisdom, see the storm coming and know it will work something good in my life?

Does He use deep distress, frozen circumstances, and chilly relationships to show me He has a better way?

Does He know that when I can't make things work on my own, I'll show up at His window sill?

He's always there, waiting for me.

Why don't I just go to Him in the first place?

Oh Lord, thank You for never giving up on me, never being too busy or forgetful, never failing to welcome me to Your perfect provision. Help me come sooner—before I try to do it all on my own. Amen

> "I will say of the LORD,
> 'He is my refuge and my fortress;
> My God, in Him I will trust.'"
> Psalm 91:2

DAY FIFTY-ONE

F.R.E.T.

"Do not fret—it only causes harm."
Psalm 37:8

Don't worry! Chill. Relax.

Easier said than done, right?

The singing king of Israel tells us three times in Psalm 37, "Do not fret." And that is exactly the kind of teaching I need: repetitious.

Merriam-Webster's Collegiate Dictionary defines fret: to cause to suffer emotional strain: VEX[2]. The Hebrew language defines the word with more sensory detail: to glow or grow warm; to blaze up, burn.

Webster's definition summons images of Elizabeth Bennett in *Pride and Prejudice.* The Hebrew version sounds more like me.

The three frets of Psalm 37 crystalized for me the day I went openly to the Lord and confessed my sin. My journal entry that morning read, "I have three bed fellows: fear, resentment, and envy."

The confession had a purging effect, as if the Lord had said to me, "Come clean." When I did, release began.

Further journal entries examined the objects of my fear, resentment, and envy, and as I wrote—a process akin to prayer for me—the recorded words of Jesus echoed in my heart:

"The truth will set you free."

Two words caught my ear—free and fret. In spelling, so close, yet miles of meanings apart.

A closer look at *fret*, and I saw an acrostic forming—fear, resentment, envy—the very things that were tormenting me. Maybe I should add *torment* and complete the crossword clue.

But when I turned to the writings of a man who understood agony and discomfort, I found the perfect word in the last two verses of his book's third chapter:

> "What I feared has come upon me;
> what I dreaded has happened to me.
> I have no peace, no quietness; I have no rest,
> but only *turmoil*."
> (Job 3:25–26 NIV)

That was the word—turmoil. Turmoil and peace cannot coexist in one's spirit. Turmoil and quietness do not walk hand in hand. Turmoil does not allude to the restful presence of God.

Turmoil ruled my heart.

If you know what it's like to heave on the waves of turmoil, keep reading tomorrow and the next day. Join me as I dig deeper into what it means to F.R.E.T.—and what it doesn't mean.

Oh God, I can bring everything to You—all my warts

and wrinkles and sins—and You love me. You loose me from those fetters and set me free. Amen.

> "Casting all your care upon Him,
> for He cares for you."
> 1 Peter 5:7

---

[2] *Merriam-Webster.com Dictionary,* s.v. "fret," accessed March 21, 2022, https://www.merriam-webster.com/dictionary/fret.

Day Fifty-Two

F Stands for Fear

> "God has not given us a spirit of fear,
> but of power and of love and of a sound mind."
> 2 Timothy 1:7

*I*n my personal acrostic of the word *fret*, fear was the first and most obvious element. I had to push it out of my life—something I could not do on my own, and that realization led to more fear. So I turned and ran straight to God's Word.

I found wonderful truths in the Bible about fear: "Perfect love casts out fear" (1 John 4:18); "I sought the Lord, and He … delivered me from all my fears" (Psalm 34:4). These tell me that God's love will chase it off and He'll snatch me from its clutches.

The breed of fear I battled was not the kind we read about when we're told to fear the Lord. There are different meanings for the word, just as there are for the word love. I love my spouse and I love lasagna. Not the same thing.

I also read the biblical stories of Sarah and how her husband's fear landed her in a harem (Genesis 12 and 20). God rescued Sarah both times. The apostle

Peter tells women they can be like Sarah if they do what is right and do not give in to fear (1 Peter 3:6). I notice the *do* and *do not* and why both are critical in the fight against fear.

The *do* part fills in the vacuum of the *do not*. Psalm 37—where I first discovered *fret*—is full of active *do* statements. Trust in the Lord and do good. Dwell, enjoy, delight, commit, be still, wait, refrain— all these in just the first eight verses.

Fear is a paralyzing poison that immobilizes us into doing nothing. Why else would lions roar? Intimidation turns their prey into a hotdog-on-a-stick.

Franklin D. Roosevelt said the only thing we have to fear is fear itself. John Wayne said courage is being scared to death and saddling up anyway.

But Jesus said, "Don't be afraid. I'm here."

In the middle of the night when all I see is darkness and all I hear is the beating of my own heart, what Jesus said wins out over the platitudes of men who once lived.

When I need help, give me the words of the God-man who *still* lives—the One who backs them up with His presence.

Thank You, Lord, for always being with me when darkness closes in and fear roars. Thank You for Your strong faithfulness. Amen.

> "Be of good cheer! It is I; do not be afraid."
> Mark 6:50

Day Fifty-Three

Suicide by Stubbornness

"Resentment kills a fool and envy slays the simple."
Job 5:2 NIV

My personal acrostic for F.R.E.T. is Fear, Resentment, Envy, and Turmoil. When I was living in the dark days of fret-induced depression, I turned to the book of Job because I wanted to read about someone else who felt beat up, someone with whom I could relate. I was stunned to find my R and E falling from the lips of one of Job's friends.

"Resentment kills a fool, and envy slays the simple" (Job 5:2 NIV). Not exactly encouraging, but worth considering. I had to admit that the very things I had been clutching were killing me. Suicide by stubbornness?

When I resent someone who has not lived up to my expectations, or resent an unforeseen situation that alters my plans, I fill up a place in my heart with poison. When I envy others who have succeeded at that to which I aspire, I add bile to the mix. A deadly concoction.

My confession broke the vials of resentment and envy, and brokenness was the big break I needed.

"Do not fret," the Lord says. "Do not fear, resent, or envy, for turmoil results."

It's a simple directive not easily carried out unless I follow God's instructions found in Psalm 37, where this whole fretful journey began for me. It tells me over and over that God is with me in my struggle, and it tells me what to do. How can I have time—or space in my heart—to fret if I am trusting, delighting, committing, listening, and waiting for Him?

For me as a writer, it was a war of words and the battlefield was the mind.

Norman Vincent Peale said, "Change your thoughts and you change your world."[3]

Ralph Waldo Emerson said, "The ancestor of every action is a thought."[4]

A hard-nosed Jewish lawyer waylaid by the living God said, "We take captive every thought to make it obedient to Christ" (2 Corinthians 10:5 NIV).

That's the winning catch phrase for me. Because of Jesus and His power, I'm no longer a prisoner fretting my life away. When I fix my mind on Christ, and remind myself of what He has said and done, I find freedom.

Thank You, God, that I don't have to fret. That in Your loving hands, brokenness is the big break I need. Thank You for Your faithfulness to put the pieces back together better than they were before. Amen.

"The sacrifices of God *are* a broken spirit,
a broken and a contrite heart—
These, O God, You will not despise."
Psalm 51:17

---

[3] "Norman Vincent Peale > Quotes > Quotable Quote," Goodreads, https://www.goodreads.com/quotes/33921-change-your-thoughts-and-you-change-your-world.

[4] "Ralph Waldo Emerson Quotes," BrainyQuote, https://www.brainyquote.com/quotes/ralphwaldoemerson_163674

Day Fifty-Four

Ready, Set, Move

> "It is not in man who walks
> to direct his own steps."
> Jeremiah 10:23

I misplaced two things during our move across town: my shoes and my Bible.

Actually, it was more than two things, because all the shoes were in one giant box because I thought it was a good idea at the time. Of course the box wasn't marked "shoes," because who marks boxes for a quickie cross-town move?

My daughter-in-law does, and it was her baby stroller or toilet box or some other box from their recent move into which I had dumped all my shoes, boots, and purses. I just couldn't remember exactly what the picture was on the outside, though I was fairly certain it wasn't the box she'd marked "Food" or "Clothes."

I padded into the cardboard forest in the garage Sunday morning in my slippers because I'd had enough foresight to set them aside. I felt like Lucy pushing through the coats in the Wardrobe.

One round through the box maze and still no shoes. I returned to the spare room that would soon be an office and dug through stacks of books looking for my Bible. I had an entire shelf of Bibles already unpacked, but I wanted *my* Bible. And I really needed shoes because that morning I was scheduled to play on the worship team. Fluffy slippers weren't going to cut it.

God tapped me on the shoulder with His wonderful sense of humor:

"And having your feet shod with the preparation of the gospel of peace …"

The only two things I needed He'd rolled up nicely in one phrase written a couple thousand years ago.

Like He knew.

After one more prayer-filled excursion through the garage, I located the baby-stroller box labeled "Towels" dead center, right under the overhead garage-door opener. I draped myself over a stack of plastic tubs and pulled out the first thing I could reach: red boots. Fine. I'd wear black jeans with them.

Sometimes we're not as prepared as we think we are.

Oh God, You *do* know! And I'm so glad. You look out for me more often than I realize and in spite of my best-laid plans. Thank You. Amen.

> "Nevertheless I am continually with You;
> You hold me by my right hand.
> You will guide me with Your counsel,
> and afterward receive me to glory."
> Psalm 73:23–24

Day Fifty-Five

Peace Like a River

> "For thus says the LORD:
> 'Behold, I will extend peace to her like a river,
> And the glory of the Gentiles like a flowing stream.
> Then you shall feed;
> On *her* sides shall you be carried,
> And be dandled on *her* knees.'"
> Isaiah 66:12

During a couple of difficult years, my husband and I lived in town—a new experience for people who had lived in the country most of their lives. But we weren't too far from the Arkansas River, and it became my saving grace.

Most mornings I loaded our Queensland heeler in the back of the Subaru and drove to the Riverwalk where Blue and I would spend an hour or so trekking along the river.

The Arkansas is a seasonal host, rushing past in early summer, swollen with snow melt and churning red or brown. In the fall it lays itself down between the yellowing cottonwoods and whispers by, laughing only in the rocky shallows or at the bulwark of the bridges.

Before my "river days," I had no idea the water was nearly a living, breathing being that spoke with many voices. One has to be right next to it, close enough to hear what it's saying. At times it roars. Some days it murmurs, and on others it shouts.

"We made it!" the river seemed to say as it passed a rocky stretch. "The rocks didn't stop us. Praise the Lord!"

If I could truly decipher the voice of the water, would I hear it speak in such a way that praises its Creator? What a beautiful declaration that would be—one to which I should add my own grateful voice.

But that's not what usually happens when I'm dashed against the boulders in my path. More often than not, I complain and grumble at what blocks my way, giving off anything but a joyous sound.

I may not have ears to hear the voice of nature, but I have no doubt it praises Him. Psalm 148 lists many things in heaven and earth that praise the Lord. When I read it, I can almost hear the water singing.

Maybe that's the secret to the peace I find when I'm in the middle of His creation at the river—the peace of praising God in all things.

Even when I'm pressed against the rocks.

Oh Lord, Your faithfulness is unending, flowing on forever like a river of life. Thank You for sharing such a peaceful reminder with me. Amen.

> "He who believes in Me, as the Scripture said, out of his heart will flow rivers of living water."
> John 7:38

Day Fifty-Six

Out of the Storm

"The L*ord* answered Job out of the whirlwind."
Job 38:1

Lightning crashed and blue light flooded the windows, blinding me with its unexpected display. Thunder shouted at the same moment, double proof that the strike was close. Possibly on our property.

I've always been fascinated by lightning storms, and in Colorado, opportunities to witness the spectacle are frequent. But when they hit close by, their power is unmistakable. Even destructive.

Outdoors is not the place to be in a lightning storm. Nor is it the optimum hideout during a tornado. Storms of any kind can be deadly.

Yet in the Old Testament we read of the prophet Ezekiel's vision of God approaching in a whirlwind of fire.

We also read of Job hearing the Lord speak to him out of a whirlwind. How close must Job have been to hear the voice of God over the roar?

I'd rather hear from God in church, where it's safe, dry, and predictable. Or from my sofa while I'm relaxing after a long day and furniture isn't flying around.

When everything is going my way is also a good time to hear from God. I love discovering His whisper when all is quiet and He fills my heart with comfort and hope.

But when God speaks to me out of the storm, there is no doubt about who's doing the talking.

No other voice can reach me above the roar of crashing hopes and plans. No one else can find me in the dream-debris or lift me from the fallen facades of my life.

No one else can calm the fear and bring peace.

He is bigger than all my storms.

And it's nice to be reminded of that.

Oh God who calmed the sea, thank You for bringing peace when my heart quakes. Amen.

> "Then He arose and rebuked the wind,
> and said to the sea, 'Peace, be still!'
> And the wind ceased and there was a great calm."
> Mark 4:39

Day Fifty-Seven

Watch Your Step

"A man's heart plans his way,
but the Lord directs his steps."
Proverbs 16:9

*T*he boxes blocked my view, stacked up in my arms three-high. They weren't heavy, just awkward, but I didn't want to carry them up from the basement one at a time. *I should be able to do this*, I thought.

Trouble is, I've never been very good at stairs when I can't see them. I've always admired people in movies—or real life—who could go tripping up and down a staircase, light on their feet, a smile on their face.

Oh, I could trip all right, just not lightly or with a smile. I had to keep my eyes on the next step so I wouldn't lose my balance and fall on my face.

Challenged with the old concrete basement stairs, I gripped the boxes tighter, tried to think perpendicularly, and planted my foot soundly on the first step. Next, the other foot, same method.

Following this approach, I soon realized what I'd not noticed before: the steps were shallower than the length of my foot. My tendency was to over-step them and jam my toes against the next one. I had to slow down, shorten my step, and concentrate on one at a time.

Since I couldn't see where I was going, I had to do this by faith, so to speak. Sounded like a spiritual metaphor I'd read somewhere.

Walking by faith is definitely harder than dashing ahead, and not nearly as fun. I like dashing ahead, running along my life path, glancing over my shoulder from time to time and yelling confidently, "Come on, Jesus. This way!"

But I don't like falling flat on my face and waiting for Him to stop and help me up—which He always does.

Hmm. Maybe I'd have more success if I slowed down and let Him lead me, just one, short footstep at a time.

God, I'm sure glad You know what we're doing and where we're going. Help me walk with You, not ahead of You. Amen.

> "For we walk by faith, not by sight."
> 2 Corinthians 5:7

DAY FIFTY-EIGHT

FROM PRESENT TO PAST AND BACK

"O LORD, our Lord,
how excellent is Your name in all the earth."
Psalm 8:1

For perhaps a couple of centuries, a natural soda spring bubbled up at a curve in the canyon west of Cañon City, Colorado, where Utes and explorers alike took the waters. The locals called it Soda Point.

In the late 1940s, someone, or many someones, decided that a paved highway was more important than the spring. That natural wonder now sleeps beneath the humming wheels of cars, pickups, and semis on US Highway 50.

Many still refer to the curve as Soda Point, and distance from it is still reckoned. Eight Mile Hill, Four Mile Creek—both places were originally measured from the Point in the mid-1800s, and they bear the same names today.

For me, Soda Point serves as a portal from the present to the past, for when I round that bend on my way to the college where I teach, I step into the world of my historical fiction.

One character, Caleb Hutton, rides his horse up the Arkansas River past Soda Point, mulling over the mistakes in his life. Discouragement dogs him until he finally learns what God can do with failure.

Though my character is fictional, the land is not, and I imagine the ochre walls and red abutments overlooking the Arkansas are much the same today as they were a hundred and fifty years ago.

I know people's struggles are the same. We still try to run from our problems rather than trust the Lord to help us work through them.

Today a steel gate blocks the path that the fictional Caleb Hutton would have taken on his ride to the mouth of the great gorge. But for those who want to see the area, there's a hiking trail along Tunnel Drive west of town, just before the turn off to Pueblo Community College's Fremont Campus. From that high vantage point, one can look out over the river and up Grape Creek where Caleb heard the "laughing waters," saw deer scaling the canyon's walls, and realized God hadn't forsaken him.

Funny, how a walk through God's creation can help us focus on His voice and His answers—whether we are reading about fictional characters or seeking God in our own very real lives.

Thank You, Lord, for Your magnificent reminders that You are still God, immovable and faithful to hear our cries for help and answer us. Amen.

> "The LORD God is my strength;
> He will make my feet like deer's feet,
> and He will make me walk on my high hills."
> Habakkuk 3:19

Day Fifty-Nine

Full of It

"And Stephen, full of faith and power,
did great wonders and signs among the people."
Acts 6:8

*W*riting Assignment: Evaluate yourself as a friend.

I instructed my college composition students one morning to measure themselves against criteria that defined a good friend, and then write a short essay supporting their findings with evidence.

Though it was a research-paper class, some students had more difficulty with spelling than anything else. As I read through their work, I found an unusual standard listed by one young man: faith fullness.

I knew he was aiming for faithfulness, but the way he wrote it made me see the term differently—perhaps with the significance he intended.

Faith fullness. According to him, a good friend was dependable and could be counted on. Someone in whom he could put his trust, hence a person who was faith full.

I wondered about my own quota. How did I measure fullness of faith? Would it be the same way I measured a tank of gas or my stomach after a satisfying meal of Italian lasagna? How about the proverbial glass of water?

Would I say I was full of faith, half full of faith, hardly at all full of faith?

I want to be full, yet Jesus said a drop the size of a mustard seed will do.

Whew! I'm so glad.

Sometimes when I look into the glass, a drop is all that's there.

God of the universe who made everything from nothing, thank You for accepting my drop of faith as something You can work with. Amen.

> "Faith is the substance of things hoped for,
> the evidence of things not seen."
> Hebrews 11:1

Day Sixty

Take My Breath Away

> "Awake, my glory!
> Awake, lute and harp!
> I will awaken the dawn."
> Psalm 57:8

My favorite time of day is sunrise, especially if I happen to catch a colorful event. I feel privileged, as if I were among the few to see such splendor.

The beautiful striations and remarkable depth of those sunrises are caused by clouds. They create the show, or rather, the sun around and through them creates the show. It has something to do with contrast—light and dark—and the glory lasts only a few minutes.

On mornings that break clear and pristine, the sun merely opens its golden eye on the land and the horizon brightens. It's beautiful, yes. An ongoing reminder of God's faithfulness, but without the pyrotechnic explosion of red and pink and orange.

It doesn't take my breath away.

I'm disappointed if morning comes to a cloudless sky because I know there won't be a show.

But that's not the way I view my life. I want *no* clouds or storms in my daily existence. No show, thank you very much.

Just give me an easy, calm, and windless life … even if the clouds and storms are the very things that magnify the power and light of the Son.

Forgive me, Lord, for wanting ease and comfort at the expense of Your beauty. Shine through the difficult dimensions of my life and display the glory of Your power. Amen.

> "I wait for the LORD, my soul waits,
> and in His word I do hope.
> My soul waits for the Lord
> more than those who watch for the morning—
> I say, more than those who watch for the morning."
> Psalm 130:5–6

Day Sixty-One

A Hiding Place

"I will say of the LORD,
He is my refuge and my fortress;
My God, in Him I will trust."
Psalm 91:2

Every time I walk along the Arkansas River, I pass a vine-draped cottonwood tree with a tent-shaped opening barely visible behind the leafy veil. Just enough mystery embraces the gnarled tree that it beckons me to come inside.

Like the lamp post in C. S. Lewis's *The Lion, the Witch, and the Wardrobe*, the scarred tree calls me into another dimension. Each time I pass it, my inner child urges me to crawl through the portal into a place where the impossible could happen.

My grown-up self sees it as a refuge where I could escape daily assaults and mundane duties.

Sometimes I just want to hide. Even in a rotted-out tree stump along the Riverwalk.

My favorite author felt the same way. David the shepherd-king wrote:

> "Rescue me from my enemies,
> O Lord, for I hide myself in You."
> (Psalm 143:9 NIV)

David's enemies were after his life. But so are mine: hurry, worry, deadlines, debt. Expectations I'll never live up to. Self-doubt, self-blame. Disappointment.

Would hiding in a tree defeat any of those enemies?

David hid in a cave, and yet it was the Lord who hid his soul and his spirit, who calmed his fears and stilled his nerves.

What better place to take cover than in the Lord God Almighty who knows everything about me and still loves me? Is there anyone or any place safer than Him?

Sometimes I need to hide.

And rest.

And soak up His strength.

And learn again like a little child that in Him, the impossible really does happen.

Oh God of the secret place, thank You for letting me hide myself in You. Amen.

> "You *are* my hiding place;
> You shall preserve me from trouble;
> You shall surround me with songs of deliverance."
> Psalm 32:7

DAY SIXTY-TWO

NEIGHBORS

> "For every beast of the forest is Mine,
> and the cattle on a thousand hills.
> I know all the birds of the mountains,
> and the wild beasts of the field are Mine."
> Psalm 50:10–11

Bears?

Here?

Yes. An adult black bear rambling up the street one night turning over trash cans and leaving deposits in the yard next door.

Last Sunday a friend from church told me she frequently spots a bruin roaming her property and sniffing her car.

"Our house backs up against open country," she said, so she's not surprised by her visitors. Just cautious.

Here along the Arkansas River, we live in a riparian habitat. That means we're not the only critters enjoying the water and shady cottonwoods. Deer, raccoons, skunks, Canada geese, herons, and mallards also make their homes nearby. So do more aggressive residents such as bobcats, bears, and cougars.

The deer are my favorite, especially a familiar doe with her twin spotted fawns. I often see them at the Riverwalk, grazing in the deeper shade of the woods, away from the trail used by people with their dogs. People like me.

Watching the gentle threesome fills me with a sense of peace and order, appreciating how God has populated His beautiful world with these marvelous creatures.

If He is taking such perfect care of these occupants of earth, won't He do the same for us? How sad when we, the crown of His creation, don't rest in His provision.

We could learn a thing or two from the critters.

Oh Lord, how magnificent is Your handiwork. May I learn, by watching Your creatures, that You faithfully provide everything I need. Amen.

> "Look at the birds of the air,
> for they neither sow nor reap nor gather into barns;
> yet your heavenly Father feeds them.
> Are you not of more value than they?"
> Matthew 6:26

Day Sixty-Three

Life Is Unfair

"For the grace of God that brings salvation
has appeared to all men."
Titus 2:11

I recently posted a fill-in-the-blank request on Facebook in the form of a question I've heard many times:

"What in the world did I ever do to deserve ____?"

I expected answers like:

Cancer
An unfaithful spouse
Losing my job

Surprisingly, not one answer was a complaint. No whining. No resentment or grumbling. Instead the answers were:

God's love and favor!
The perfect children that God blessed me with
Such a cool and thoughtful Auntie!

My beautiful family
All the blessings this life has given me
The Lord's love and protection … beyond understanding
Mercy
My sweet hubby and darling daughter
Jesus
Grace

One respondent said he knew it was a loaded question. That's good. It means he has already confronted himself with what matters most in the face of life's unfairness. And it is unfair, you know.

I haven't done one single thing to deserve the privilege of walking along the river on a clear morning, or marveling at the beauty of a silent snowfall, or coming home to a warm house and a hot cup of coffee. I've done nothing to deserve my family and good health, a job I enjoy, faithful friends, or God's grace and forgiveness.

But I'm thankful for it all.

Yes, life is unfair. And I am extremely grateful that I don't get what I deserve.

Thank You, God, for not giving me what I deserve but graciously giving me what I don't deserve. Amen.

> "For by grace you have been saved through faith,
> and that not of yourselves;
> it is the gift of God, not of works,
> lest anyone should boast."
> Ephesians 2:8–9

Day Sixty-Four

Going It Alone—Or Not

> "Two are better than one,
> because they have a good reward for their labor."
> Ecclesiastes 4:9

The first morning I saw the white-haired couple on the Riverwalk, I nearly stared. Not because of their age, but because of their unified presence.

The woman wore a thin clear tube around her head that delivered oxygen to her nose from a portable canister. Her male companion wore the canister.

He also held the woman's hand, walking in step with her so the hose was never stretched or crimped.

In his other hand he held a red-tipped white cane.

He was blind.

They strode along the trail together as if they were forty years younger and in perfect health.

The woman did the seeing, the man did the breathing, in a sense. I suppose she could have carried her own oxygen supply and he could have tapped his cane from side to side, but their cooperative effort in helping one another was a beautiful thing to behold.

Rare.

They had chosen to be dependent upon each other and were, therefore, more confident—a picture of what dependence can mean. How two can be stronger than one.

When Jesus sent out his disciples, He sent them by twos (see Mark 6:7). Could this have been reflective of His Father's decree that it wasn't good for man to be alone?

I doubt the man and woman on the Riverwalk would argue that principle. They chose to not walk alone and had perfected their coupled pace.

Independence, in the personal sense, often leaves much to be desired.

Often I am by myself, but I'm never alone. I'd hate to be walking this road of life on my own.

Oh Lord, thank You for telling us that You will never leave us or forsake us. Thank You for never leaving us alone. Amen.

> "For if they fall, one will lift up his companion.
> But woe to him who is alone when he falls,
> for he has no one to help him up."
> Ecclesiastes 4:10

Day Sixty-Five

Perspective

"Not that I speak in regard to need,
for I have learned in whatever state I am,
to be content."
Philippians 4:11

Park rangers may have set the flat stones in a stairstep pattern that curved up the small rise, but whoever it was, I appreciated their efforts.

The path led to a lonely juniper standing boldly against a piercingly blue sky. A picturesque pose just asking to be photographed.

I climbed the stone-slab steps, but when I reached the top, the picture changed dramatically, for the juniper was gnarled and knotted, anything but elegant.

It grew literally out of the rock formation, leaning sideways, parallel to the ground, and its branches shot skyward from its twisted trunk. Not at all the lovely tree I had perceived from below.

From my higher perspective, the juniper's curving trunk framed a cluster of golden cottonwoods across the draw, flaming along a mountain creek. Yet as beautiful as they were, the cottonwoods did not inspire me like the old, weathered conifer.

The cottonwoods grew easily by the water, unencumbered and unopposed. The juniper had fought a lengthy battle to survive its location. It showed me that the rock and the hard place could also be fertile ground.

I knew what it felt like to be stuck between a rock and a hard place. The tongue-in-cheek cliché is typically a go-to phrase when times are tough.

When I feel wedged in a difficult situation, pressed upon by immovable obstacles and opposition, I begin to doubt that I can do what I thought I was called to do. Other people are so much better at what I aspire to. Why should I push against the hard place? Why should I try?

But God is not hampered in His purposes by mere surroundings. And sometimes He has to move me to change my perspective. It's then I see the possibilities in situations I never would have seen otherwise.

Lord, please help me to not underestimate Your ability to use me wherever I am, wherever You have placed me, whether it is lovely or lonely. Thank You for Your provision in whatever my surroundings may be. Amen.

> "I can do all things through Christ
> who strengthens me."
> Philippians 4:13

DAY SIXTY-SIX

IS THIS GOOD ENOUGH?

"You shall love the LORD your God with all your heart,
with all your soul, and with all your mind."
Matthew 22:37

For years I have told my own children and students that there is no such thing as a stupid question. I've changed my mind.

Too many times one of those aforementioned youngsters posed the query, "Is this good enough?"

The answer is always no.

Okay, maybe it's not a *stupid* question like, "How much do you weigh?" But it's certainly an annoying and unnecessary question.

In the context of effort, "good enough" insinuates that whatever "it" is could be better. "Good enough" usually means the inquisitor wants me to settle for something less than his best.

Students asking if their writing assignment is good enough are really saying their formatting could be better and the story could be longer. My son and daughter asking if the results of their chores are good enough are telling me the toilet could be cleaner, the leaf bags fuller, and some of the bowls in the dishwasher were facing up, not down.

I'm not saying every result must be perfect. Perfectionism drives people away and leaves the perfectionist frustrated. A six-year-old cannot accomplish what a sixteen-year-old can, nor should she be required to do so. But every effort should be one's best. No halfhearted attempts.

Please don't confuse this idea with the advertising world's lure that we need bigger, more expensive products. Bigger is not always better, and more is not always best. But when it comes to giving, sharing, working, and helping, "good enough" shortchanges the whole process.

Something is missing.

I want to give God my best, not my almost-best. Every day He gives me twenty-four hours. Never once has He asked, "Are twenty enough?"

At creation, God said, "Let there be light," not "Let there be just enough light."

And on His way to Calvary, Jesus didn't pause, look up from beneath the cross's weight and say, "Is this close enough?"

My best won't be flawless because I am an imperfect human. But I don't want to fall back on halfheartedness. Why offer a good-enough effort when I can give the finest that I have?

Lord, thank You for giving me Your very best—so much better than I can give You, and yet You accept what I *can* give. Myself. Amen.

"And do not be conformed to this world,
but be transformed by the renewing of your mind,
that you may prove what is that good and acceptable
and perfect will of God."
Romans 12:2

Day Sixty-Seven

No Secondhand Days

"Through the Lord's mercies we are not consumed,
because His compassions fail not.
They are new every morning."
Lamentations 3:22–23

I love a good bargain. And I love finding surprises in unexpected places like thrift stores and garage sales. Those discoveries make me feel like the Proverbs 31 woman who brings her treasures from afar.

But when I looked out the window above my desk this morning, I realized that God isn't always that thrifty. He doesn't look for a good deal or wait for a sale. Of course I saw the same old juniper bushes and blue spruce tree, and the distant Wet Mountains wore their familiar dark cloak of pine. But the day itself was unique. Brand new.

God had done it again. He gave us a brand-new, never-been-used-before morning.

There are no secondhand days with God. He doesn't scrimp or pinch pennies but goes all out on everything He touches.

If the Creator had only one day to give us, I believe He would have. I base that judgment upon how He's handled other valuable gifts, particularly His Son.

God has one perfect Son, Jesus, and He gave Him for our imperfect lives. Do we even begin to understand the depth of that giving?

Not only do we have brand-new lives because of Jesus, we have a sparkling, new hope because of Him.

And we have never-been-used-before mornings for which to praise Him, every single day.

Now there's something to be thankful for.

Life-giver God, how generous You are with Your love and Your gifts. Thank You for sending Jesus—and every brand-new sunrise. Amen.

> "Every good and perfect gift is from above,
> and comes down from the Father of lights,
> with whom there is no variation
> or shadow of turning."
> James 1:17

Day Sixty-Eight

Only the Clean and Unbroken

"Create in me a clean heart, O God,
And renew a steadfast spirit within me."
Psalm 51:10

I drove past the local flower shop and cringed when I read the sign: "Only the Clean and Unbroken."

I knew the store owner was recycling floral vases and encouraging people to bring them in rather than throw them away. And I knew the sign referred to the inexpensive glass containers used to deliver bouquets and rosebuds.

But somehow the words felt like a personal indictment: I was anything but clean and unbroken.

Oh God, I thought. *What if You required me to be unsoiled and whole before coming to You? What would I do with the stained and broken pieces of my life?*

Israel's great shepherd-king wrote, "The sacrifices of God are a broken spirit; a broken and a contrite heart—these, O God, You will not despise" (Psalm 51:17). When King David cried out in this psalm, he was a broken and sin-stained man. He had not only stolen another man's wife, but also had that man killed. As a result, an innocent child died. Not exactly a pristine situation.

However, David knew he could run to his God in spite of the blood on his hands and the blackness of his heart. He knew the Lord would look on his brokenness and repentance and forgive him, wash him, and make him whole again.

Centuries later when Jesus was accused by religious leaders of hanging out with the riff-raff, he replied, "Those who are well have no need of a physician, but those who are sick. I did not come to call the righteous, but sinners, to repentance" (Mark 2:17).

God is in the recycling business, but unlike the local florist, He restores and recycles human wreckage. He wants to use us again, but first He will do what we cannot: put us back together and wash us with the sin-cleansing blood of Jesus.

Oh Lord, thank You that I don't have to clean myself up before I can come to You—that You take me as I am, and promise to make me new. Amen.

> "Behold, I make all things new."
> Revelation 21:5

Day Sixty-Nine

On My Own

> "Though he fall, he shall not be utterly cast down;
> for the LORD upholds him with His hand."
> Psalm 37:24

When my granddaughter Hadley was a toddler, I watched her one day a week.

She slowed me down, thank God.

She drew my focus to tiny hands, the floor I thought was clean, the lower shelves of my bookcase. She forced me to look at things from a different perspective. And she demonstrated a reckless determination.

As a new walker, she fell on her padded bottom countless times. Toddling around the house much faster than she should have, she would trip over a loose throw rug or a toy she didn't see. And she repeatedly snagged her chubby feet on the corner of the blanket she insisted on dragging, much like the Peanuts' character, Linus.

But she never gave up. She just kept *getting* up.

I am a lot like my granddaughter. How often do I charge straight ahead without looking where I'm going? How many times have I tripped over an unnoticed obstacle and fallen spiritually or emotionally?

I don't get up as quickly as she did. Sometimes I just lie there for a minute and moan. After all, my landing spot is a little farther away for me than it was for her.

However, I too have someone watching over me, checking things out from my perspective, understanding exactly what it's like to be in my shoes—or bare feet. And He loves me even more than I love my granddaughter. Hard to imagine, isn't it?

When I picked up that little bundle of wiggles to comfort her or listen to her frustrated, evolving language, I was reminded that the Lord does the same for me.

Oh God, how faithful You are to pick me up and comfort me, no matter how many times I stumble. Help me always remember to run to You when I fall.

> "As one whom his mother comforts,
> so I will comfort you."
> Isaiah 66:13

Day Seventy

Ready or Not

> "For the Son of Man has come to seek
> and to save that which was lost."
> Luke 19:10

Remember playing the childhood game Hide and Seek or Hide and Go Seek? We ran away from the seeker who closed his eyes and counted to ten while we squeezed under any little bush or board we could find.

"Ready or not, here I come!" the seeker yelled.

Life is like that when we grow up. Most of us think we are well hidden. Truth is, we're not. Those six little words of warning pop out at the most unexpected moments:

Root canals.

Divorce.

Death.

Some things find us whether we are ready for them or not.

I was reminded of this fact when we totaled our car on a rainy, midnight highway. All of my so-called preparation of water, a blanket, and a flashlight in the trunk meant little. I forgot all about them as I groped in the back seat for my flying cell phone and the glasses that were moments before resting comfortably on my face.

My husband and I survived the crash, the airbags, and the insurance delays, but since then my emergency kit has expanded to include first aid, a toothbrush, and deodorant—those niceties we take for granted until holed up in a roadside motel without them. Fortunately, I get another go at "ready or not."

We don't get a second go at eternity. It's a one-shot deal and there's only one exit.

My husband and I were spiritually ready that night, for we are both hidden *and* found in Jesus because He came to find and save the lost. The rescue is based on His work, not ours.

All my good deeds are mere afterthoughts compared to His mercy. They are wonderful things, but not as wonderful as His saving grace. When I look into forever, they will be only as good as water, blankets, and flashlights in the trunk.

How about you? Have you found forgiveness in Jesus? Better yet, have you found Him? He isn't lost, and He's not hiding. He's the Seeker, and will someday shout through the heavens, "Ready or not, here I come."

Thank You, Lord, for finding us and hiding us in You. Amen.

> "Yet indeed I also count all things loss
> for the excellence of the knowledge
> of Christ Jesus my Lord,
> for whom I have suffered the loss of all things ...
> that I may gain Christ and be found in Him."
> Philippians 3:8–9

DAY SEVENTY-ONE

OUT OF CONTROL

"In the world you will have tribulation;
but be of good cheer,
I have overcome the world."
John 16:33

A small natural disaster created a major inconvenience here the other day. On national radar it was a blip; locally it was a rockslide.

Literally.

Seven thousand tons of rock slipped off the mountain and across US Highway 50 like a string of broken beads. The twenty-foot swath closed the two-lane road west of Cañon City for nearly a week. Commuters, tourists, and delivery trucks had to reroute more than a hundred miles out of their way.

Twenty feet doesn't seem like much, roughly the length of a modern living room. But when individual rocks are themselves twenty feet across, there's no getting around the issue.

Road crews broke, blasted, and drilled the boulders into more manageable chunks before loading them onto semis. Three hundred truck loads later, traffic again flowed along the main artery that courses through Colorado's Arkansas River canyon.

It doesn't take much to stop our forward progress: downsizing, a disabled refrigerator, rumors of war. Death.

How startling to discover that we are not in control after all.

How dare those rocks slide into our path. How dare our boss fire us. How dare we get sick now when we're so busy.

How dare the carefully threaded beads of our lives come tumbling down around our feet and roll away.

And how glad I am—truly—that it's not all up to me after all.

Oh, God what would I do without You? Thank You for being bigger than anything that happens in my world and for having my eternal interest at heart. Amen.

> "Cast all your anxiety on him
> because he cares for you."
> 1 Peter 5:7 NIV

Day Seventy-Two

Spiritual Backbone

"Therefore I desire that the men pray everywhere, lifting up holy hands, without wrath and doubting."
1 Timothy 2:8

When I last visited a chiropractor, he demonstrated for me the reason many people suffer back pain and stiffness.

"It's all about posture," he said.

I thought I knew what he was going to say next, because I've heard it since I was a kid: "Sit up straight."

But the chiropractor surprised me with a more vivid application. Sitting on the edge of a chair, he curled into himself, drooped his arms and shoulders forward, hunched his back, and dropped his head.

"This is how people sit," he said, barely audible in his curved position.

"And this is how they should sit."

With that, he raised his head, straightened his back, and lifted both arms as if opening himself up to the world or the sky or ... God. It was a perfect position of praise.

Even in the physical world, we see a picture of a healthier spiritual posture: open, looking up, arms wide to receive the blessings of God.

This little display made me wonder how my spirit looks to the Mender of my soul. Am I turned in upon myself, or am I open, looking upward in expectancy, praising Him for all He's done and is about to do?

Perhaps a little more praise and gratitude will improve my gaze and attitude, and give me the stronger spiritual backbone that I need.

Oh God, Your messages are everywhere! I need only to look around and see a hint of Your purpose and wisdom. Thank You for such clarity. Amen.

> "Therefore strengthen the hands which hang down, and the feeble knees."
> Hebrews 12:12

DAY SEVENTY-THREE

PROCRASTINATION

"Behold, now is the accepted time;
behold, now is the day of salvation."
2 Corinthians 6:2

After driving our pickup home on icy roads with blowing snow and a semi bearing down on me, I had a much deeper appreciation for the phrase "white-knuckling it." I was just grateful to make it to our driveway without sliding off the highway or adorning the hood of the semi.

Snow has been called the Great Equalizer. It slows everyone, covers everyone. All of us are the same: travelers struggling to make it safely to our destinations, whether in semis or pickups.

As much as I loved the beauty of the falling flakes, I'll admit I groused about dashing through them from the parking lot to the grocery store that day. I had taken the pickup without much thought of the forecast, so I didn't take a muffler. Or an umbrella. Or an extra coat in the back seat.

I live in Colorado. I knew better.

Remember when your mother said, "Never put off until tomorrow what you can do today"? People credit Thomas Jefferson with those words, but it was probably his mother. A woman who would say, "Don't put off getting your glasses fixed. Do it today, not tomorrow."

Well, I didn't. I put off going into town that Friday because I was going in on Saturday, so why make an extra trip just for my glasses?

But I didn't get them fixed on Saturday either because the temperature dropped thirty degrees in thirty minutes and a blizzard blew in hours before it was predicted.

Guess who spent three days trying to read and work at the computer in a white-out?

Procrastination cost me a lot, but it also gave me something in return: blurred vision and a killer headache.

Some people put off going to the doctor. Others put off saving money, exercising, eating right, or talking to God.

Snow isn't the only equalizer, so is time. We don't get tomorrow. We think we do, but by the time it gets here, it's today.

Whatever it is we need to do, from saving money to talking to God, we should start today. It's really the only time we have.

Thank You, God, for the miracle of time even though it's always faster or slower than I want. You knew I couldn't handle everything at once. Help me prioritize by tending to the important things and not putting off those for which I may not get a second chance. Amen.

"Do not boast about tomorrow,
for you do not know what a day may bring forth."
Proverbs 27:1

Day Seventy-Four

The Medicine Train

> "Now in the morning,
> having risen a long while before daylight,
> He went out and departed to a solitary place;
> and there He prayed."
> Mark 1:35

The train wrapped around an approaching curve, and from our seats in the dining car, my husband and I watched the engines of the *California Zephyr* disappear.

On the first day of our two-day journey from Denver to Sacramento, the train laced through snowy canyons and stretched across narrow valleys tucked deep in the Rocky Mountains. A perfect beginning to eight wintry days off the grid.

Time jumped the track.

I remembered what I'd forgotten—that I could live without the virtual umbilical cord of instant communication and information from people I know and don't know.

I learned that I could sit on a train and feed my soul on scenery seen by very few.

I realized that God is not imprisoned in seconds and minutes, hours and days.

Be still
and know
that I
am God.

The gentle rhythm of the rails drew the words through my heart like the *Zephyr* through the canyons.

I was not required to drive, watch for traffic, get directions from Siri, or find a place to stop for lunch. I did nothing. Nothing but enjoy my husband's company and the view. I've never been very good at doing nothing, but this time, I excelled.

Family met us at the train station in Sacramento. With no particular agenda, we dined with our daughter the first day, drove to the coast the following and spent time with our nearly-adult grandchildren. Another day we met with a friend from our own youth.

On Sunday we worshipped at a church by the sea, rode bicycles along Cannery Row, and shared conversations that drew us closer and prepared us for—

—the roaring engines of an airliner that brought us home in a crowded tube of harried people with crying children and frazzled parents.

At home in my office, 381 email messages awaited. Amazing how the internet had churned on without me during those eight days—and how I settled and relaxed without it.

"The train was like medicine," my husband said the day after our return. A miracle out of time that reminded us both how close God is if we will stop and listen, wait and watch.

Oh Lord, You renew our faith and give us fresh hope when we take time away from the noise and spend it with You. Thank You. Amen.

> "Be still, and know that I am God."
> Psalm 46:10

Day Seventy-Five

Resistance

"My brethren,
count it all joy when you fall into various trials,
knowing that the testing of your faith
produces patience.
But let patience have its perfect work,
that you may be perfect and complete,
lacking nothing."
James 1:2–4

I have Mom Arms. You know, those upper limbs that come complete with built-in bat wings. I'm beginning to understand why my mother never wore sleeveless shirts in public.

As a writer, I do more heavy sitting than heavy lifting and my biceps and triceps have atrophied. Not the skin surrounding them, however.

Exercise is important for a balanced life, I know this, but I detest going to the gym. I just can't bring myself to drive into town so I can work up a sweat with people I don't know, slinging dead weight around and trying to hold my stomach in at the same time.

So I walk. Most mornings before sunrise, I tramp out a two-mile hike up the road and back again. But that doesn't help my arms.

Recently, my son The Body-Builder put together a home-front workout regimen for me based on his experience as a personal trainer.

"Resistance is what you want," he explained. Demonstrating with a long rubber jump rope I bought years ago, he stood on the band with a handle from each end in each hand, and effortlessly stretched his arms skyward.

"Keep your elbows close to your head, and push slowly upward."

I'm good at slowly. I barely moved, so he showed me how to reduce the resistance for now and how to increase it later as my strength improves.

I don't enjoy this resistance-training thing, but I know what little strength I have left will fade even more if I don't do it. God knows it too, and He uses the human body as a great object lesson for the human spirit. I like the explanation found in *The Message* about becoming "mature and well-developed, not deficient in any way" (James 1:4 MSG).

Mature I've got down. Well-developed, not so much. If that's how I want my arms (and spirit) to look, I need to get busy on the resistance training. With a smile.

Thank You, Lord, for giving me easy-to-understand examples of how difficulties strengthen me. Help me keep smiling. Amen.

"We also glory in tribulations,
knowing that tribulation produces perseverance;
and perseverance, character; and character, hope."
Romans 5:3–4

DAY SEVENTY-SIX

SHOW, DON'T TELL

> "Show me your faith without your works,
> and I will show you my faith by my works."
> James 2:18

In the spring, Canada geese spend their days along the Arkansas River teaching their goslings how to be geese. But Mom and Dad don't stand on the shore squawking orders like the famous insurance-mascot duck.

They simply go about their daily routine while their little puff-ball offspring watch and copy, doing what they see the grownups doing. The elders are showing, not telling—a feat which embodies the standing mantra in the writer's world.

"Show, Don't Tell."

The first time I heard this directive, I didn't understand. How can a writer show *without* telling since words are all he has?

I soon learned the difference. Which sentence below *shows* what the woman is feeling?

1. She was so angry she could have choked him.
2. She squeezed her fingers around the arms of her chair rather than his throat.

Number 2 is the correct answer because a picture is worth a thousand words. People evidently prefer show over tell or the thousand-word cliché would not be cliché.

A recent guest speaker at our church picked up on the writer's catch phrase and proved that it's nothing new.

"Show them, don't just tell them," he said of sharing our faith with others.

A couple thousand years ago a man named James pressed a similar point when he said, "I will show you my faith by my works."

And roughly a thousand years later, a Franciscan monk from Assisi is thought to have put it even more succinctly: "Preach the Gospel always. If necessary, use words."

Others have said, "Put your money where your mouth is," implying that "talk is cheap."

I think they're right.

Lord, help me work on my "show, don't tell" where faith and Christianity are concerned. Help me show others what I believe. Amen.

"For I was hungry and you gave Me food;
I was thirsty and you gave Me drink;
I was a stranger and you took Me in;
I was naked and you clothed Me;
I was sick and you visited Me;
I was in prison and you came to Me …
Inasmuch as you did it to one of the least of these
My brethren, you did it to Me."
Matthew 25:35–36, 40

Day Seventy-Seven

Unimproved Road

> "These things I have spoken to you,
> that in me you may have peace.
> In the world you will have tribulation;
> but be of good cheer,
> I have overcome the world."
> John 16:33

"UNIMPROVED ROAD," the yellow, diamond-shaped sign said.

Looked all right to me. Just a typical country lane.

My husband and I continued along the unpaved road through grazing land and open cow country, admiring an old ranch house and barn surrounded by towering cottonwood trees. The beautiful setting inspired peaceful thoughts as we drove on toward a friend's secluded mountain home.

A hard right turn, and the road roughened a bit with a few more dips and rises. Another half mile and the path narrowed. Rocks replaced gravel as roadbed, and I felt like I was in one of those off-road, he-man truck commercials.

A long drop quickly turned into a steep climb up the other side, and we didn't dare stop for fear of getting stuck right where we were. The term *roadbed* deteriorated into *gouge,* but we trooped on.

Unimproved proved to be the understatement of the year.

But we'd been warned.

Once we made it up to the pine-covered plateau, our friend's home beckoned just ahead. The view of the valley floor we'd crossed and the higher mountains beyond was staggering.

The destination was definitely worth the journey.

Our friends drove that road every day—in a Subaru just like ours. That knowledge had encouraged us that we could do it too, and we did.

Jesus offers the same kind of encouragement. He said we'd have trouble in this world and He was right. He gave us fair warning, but He didn't stop there.

He's done this. He walked a similar, if not tougher, road. It's hard, but it's worth it, and we'll make it because He goes with us.

Rather than letting the ups and downs of life discourage us, let's not only take heart, but take Him at His word.

Lord, thank You for Your faithfulness to walk beside us in this life, rather than sit back and watch us struggle on our own. Amen.

> "For He Himself has said,
> 'I will never leave you nor forsake you.'"
> Hebrews 13:5

DAY SEVENTY-EIGHT

TMI!

> "The nations raged,
> the kingdoms were moved."
> Psalm 46:6

*T*oo much information—the clamor was killing me!

I wanted to run screaming from my computer and all the visual noise of earthquakes, floods, celebrity divorces, politics, and over-paid athletes. Would it never end?

As a matter of fact, it did. As soon as I turned off the internet and the television.

I picked up my Bible and began reading Psalm 46.

"God is our refuge and strength ..." Ah, yes. That was what I needed.

Yet soon the turmoil returned. The earth had shaken, the waters roared and foamed, and mountains trembled with the surging as a small nation suffered devastation.

The psalm shifted again, following the up and down of my modern world, and for a brief interlude, I saw a peaceful river flowing through the City of God before things churned up anew.

Destructive images brought to mind the Middle East, Afghanistan, and Ukraine before God stepped in to break the bow, shatter the spear, and burn the shields with fire.

And following was the answer: "Be still, and know that I am God" (v. 10).

Could this be what I needed, to simply still my heart and the noise in my life? Could these ancient words apply even to my modern existence?

Thank God, yes.

Regardless of what nature sends, regardless of how men and nations boast and threaten and stage themselves, God is still God.

Still waiting for me.

Still there.

Still.

And when I still myself, I hear Him over the noise, deep in my heart.

Thank You, God, for Your faithfulness, for seeing us through the turmoil, and rescuing us from distraction. Amen.

> "God is our refuge and strength,
> A very present help in trouble."
> Psalm 46:1

DAY SEVENTY-NINE

YOU ARE WORTH THE WAIT

"He who has begun a good work in you
will complete it until the day of Jesus Christ."
Philippians 1:6

After completing another draft of my inspirational romantic-suspense novel, I laid it aside to let it simmer. In a few weeks, I'll go back to it with fresh eyes and work through it again.

The manuscript is not perfect. I need to grind down a few rough spots, flesh out certain scenes—do the whole nip-and-tuck thing. I will cut away entire sections and breathe life into others. It's not ready for the publisher, but I'm not giving up on it. I believe in it.

I believe in the story's message: that Christ cares about individuals. Jesus went out of His way here on earth to talk to people one-on-one and I believe He still does. He continues to impart peace through His presence by the Holy Spirit.

Considering the value I place on the story I've written, I'm not a bit surprised by my near-parental zeal for it. Could that be a picture of how God feels about me? After all, I am His work. His creation.

I am not perfect. I have emotional rough edges ready for grinding, attitudes that need to be fleshed out and others that should be surgically removed. But based on what He says in His Word, He believes in me. He's not giving up on me. I am not yet complete, but by the time He's finished, I will be.

Someday I'll be published in paradise. God will say, "Look what I did. Look what My Son's blood bought and purified."

I am His workmanship, created in Christ Jesus.

So are you.

Don't give up on yourself.

He hasn't.

Thank You, God, for believing in me. Thank You for not tossing me on the discard pile and starting over with something else. Thank You for giving Your all to complete me. Amen.

> "For we are His workmanship,
> created in Christ Jesus for good works,
> which God prepared beforehand
> that we should walk in them."
> Ephesians 2:10

DAY EIGHTY

WHICH VOICE?

> "Day unto day utters speech,
> and night unto night reveals knowledge.
> There is no speech nor language
> where their voice is not heard."
> Psalm 19:2–3

Voices from the phone in my pocket tell me the weather outside is miserable and I have messages waiting to be answered.

Voices from the box of windows on my desk tell me the world is out of control, peace is impossible, and the future is bleak. They shout about the government, the economy, and the industry I'm involved in. They tell me that evil is on the rise and justice is on the lam. That I need a newer car, a smaller figure, and a bigger house.

A discouraging thirty minutes of online headline news, endless email, and doomsday articles nearly send me spiraling. What a way to start the day.

Usually I don't. I like to hear the quiet first, but some days I jump right in. Thankfully, I can jump right out … outside for a walk with the dog, up a gently climbing road bordered by hay fields that stretch for miles.

Flocks of red-winged blackbirds cling to wild yellow sunflowers, plucking seeds and chirping as the sun lifts over the nearest hill.

All the electronic voices fade away. Tension eases. I see the morning brighten—and my heart responds.

A different voice says,

"I've got this."

So which of the voices should I heed? Which voice will I let lead?

I'd rather listen to the Voice that spoke before time and created light. The Voice that calmed a stormy sea and fear-filled hearts. The Voice that reminds me that He is in control.

Even without technology—*especially* without technology—I can hear the comforting voice of God, and I know it's all going to work out.

Oh Lord, I'm so glad You've got this. Amen.

> "Where morning dawns, where evening fades,
> you call forth songs of joy."
> Psalm 65:8 NIV

DAY EIGHTY-ONE

WHAT'S YOUR POV?

"Behold, the eye of the LORD is on
those who fear Him,
On those who hope in His mercy."
Psalm 33:18

POV—point of view. It is critical to an author.

As a story unfolds, whose viewpoint will a writer use to describe a scene – the hero or the heroine? From which character's perspective does he want the reader to view the action or feel the angst?

While writing a particularly emotional scene in one of my books, I wasn't sure which character had the most important perspective, so I wrote the scene twice—once from the hero's point of view and once from the heroine's point of view. I had to get into each character's head as I wrote, and the scene was different through each character's eyes. I wanted only one in the book, so I used the POV of the character who had more to lose if things went wrong.

Authors typically pick one viewpoint in relating specific scenes such as a chase, an argument, or a tender moment, and it makes a difference to the reader.

Remember high school debate class when we had to argue on the side we didn't agree with? We were forced to consider someone else's perspective or point of view.

Objects take on different colors and contours when viewed from different angles. So do situations, lives.

Because we are finite, personally motivated creatures, we don't often see the big picture. We can't crane our neck around the next bend, and often miss the other guy's viewpoint.

Sometimes we think no one sees ours.

But God does. He sees the lily, the sparrow, and the panting deer. He sees the blind man begging and the woman weeping. He sees tomorrow.

Take a trek through the Gospels and count how many times Jesus looks at someone. Really looks. Sees them. Can you feel His compassionate Creator-eyes on you?

God sees us and loves us. He sees and loves others too. Maybe if we sought His perspective more often, we'd understand ourselves and other people better.

Maybe we need a little less of our own POV and more of His.

Oh Lord, give me eyes to see people from Your perspective of compassion. Teach me to see them as You see me—with love. Amen.

"Then [Hagar] called the name of the Lord
who spoke to her,
You-Are-the-God-Who-Sees; for she said,
'Have I also here seen Him who sees me?'"
Genesis 16:13

DAY EIGHTY-TWO

CHARACTER

"Behold, to obey is better than sacrifice,
and to heed than the fat of rams."
1 Samuel 15:22

As a writing instructor, I teach workshop participants how to show their characters' personalities rather than simply tell about them.

Someone wiser than I summed up the principle by saying, "Actions speak louder than words."

Using this approach in reverse, I've lately been considering Moses—the biblical character portrayed by Charlton Heston in Cecil B. DeMille's movie *The Ten Commandments*. Heston's larger-than-life personality was easy to believe, but when I observe Moses as recorded in Old Testament accounts, his actions show me a fallible man, imperfect in spite of his position as a national leader.

Moses had grown up in the house of an Egyptian Pharaoh, yet his rage over an apparent injustice to a Hebrew slave drove him to kill an Egyptian task master and hide the body.

Cold case, anyone?

Years later, after countless hours alone in God's presence on Mount Sinai, Moses' rage got the better of him again, and he smashed a couple of God-inscribed stone tablets when he found his people slipping back into their old pagan ways.

Temper, temper, Moses.

Surprisingly, I've not found that God reprimanded him for either incident, though I'm sure the Creator does not condone murder or tantrums.

But Moses's temper finally led to disobedience in a seemingly small matter after the wandering Jews complained yet again of not having enough water. Their parents had done the same forty years earlier, and God had told Moses to strike a rock at Horeb and water would gush out.

Again God tells Moses how to quench the people's thirst, but Moses is to speak to the rock in Kadesh, not strike it.

Pause for a moment and consider Moses. *Been there*, done that, he must have thought. *I hit a rock once before and got water. This time I'll really blast it and knock those crybabies off their feet!*

Could it have been Moses's bent to anger that led him to hit the rock—twice—instead of speaking to it? A small matter, we think, but not to God.

"Because you didn't trust Me," God told Moses, "and revere Me in front of these people, you won't be going to that land I promised them."

Murder and tantrums paled in the glare of disobedience.

No doubt, my actions reveal my character to those around me as well. If Israel's great Law Giver couldn't keep his act together, where does that leave me?

It leaves me at the mercy seat of Jesus. Thank God He made a way for us in our imperfection. If He hadn't, we wouldn't make it to Him.

Thank You, God, for the mercy You gave us in the sacrifice of Your Son. Without it, I would be doomed. Amen.

> "For this is the love of God,
> that we keep His commandments.
> And His commandments are not burdensome."
> 1 John 5:3

DAY EIGHTY-THREE

THE POTTER

> "But indeed, O man,
> who are you to reply against God:
> Will the thing formed say to him who formed it,
> 'Why have you made me like this?'"
> Romans 9:20

I heard a dull thump as I entered the church Sunday morning. Like a heavy heart thrown against the floor.

I wasn't far off.

A potter stood near the edge of the platform with a large block of red clay in his hands and slammed it onto the tarp-covered stage. Then he picked it up and slammed it down again.

I shuddered.

I knew the Old Testament account of God sending Jeremiah to the potter's house. I liked the part about the artisan creating a usable vessel. I didn't like what I saw at the moment.

Our guest speaker had to soften the cold, unyielding clay, make it pliable before he could use it. The force of his throw surprised me. Justified. Focused. Fierce.

The Bible story hadn't mentioned this part.

The potter seated himself behind his wheel, the mound of clay in its center. He set the wheel spinning, dipped his hands in a bowl of water, and wrapped his fingers around the lump, smoothing it upward, downward, dipping again in the water and returning to the clay.

His slightest impression made a rim at the top, and with the press of his fingers, the clay slowly cratered. He drew the sides upward and out.

All this time he spoke of how God had worked in his life, how He had carried him through divorce and loneliness, out of darkness and into light. Into marriage again. Into ministry. The potter's voice soothed us as gently as his fingers smoothed the clay that transformed before our eyes.

Patience and pressure created a large bowl from the formless lump. Just the right amount of water, just the right speed of the wheel, just the right movement of the potter's fingers. I was transfixed by the miracle, yet unprepared for what he did next.

Finished with the bowl, he rose from his seat and picked up an unfired vase from a nearby pedestal, still the dark copper color of workable clay. He turned the vase in his hands, revealing the other side, disfigured by jagged cuts that made it unfit to use.

And then he wrapped his arms around the piece and pressed it to his body, crushing it against his chest. The vase collapsed in his embrace, and he folded it over and into itself.

He would remake it, he said. Nothing would be lost. Nothing wasted. It would be a thing of beauty and purpose again.

In that moment I felt the gentle pressure of fingers on my heart. And I understood the hope of healing at the touch of the Potter's hand.

Oh God of healing hands, make my heart anew. Amen.

> "Arise and go down to the potter's house,
> and there I will cause you to hear My words."
> Jeremiah 18:2

Day Eighty-Four

Chewing On the Bread of Life

"Be diligent to present yourself approved to God,
a worker who does not need to be ashamed,
rightly dividing the word of truth."
2 Timothy 2:15

I recently signed a contract to write content for a popular devotional guide. The publisher will choose the Scripture references, send them to me, and I am to come up with the application and commentary.

Suddenly, the idea of commenting on the Bible seemed rather presumptuous. Who was I to offer my opinion or interpretation of what God said?

"Lord," I prayed one morning from my quiet-time spot on the sofa. "I would never presume to add to Your Word. Help me!"

In the calm of that moment, a clear message came to mind: *Rightly divide the word of truth.*

Oh. Yeah, I'd read that, hadn't I?

Just as suddenly as doubt had come, so came an image of Jesus dividing fish and small loaves of bread and telling His disciples to distribute the pieces to a hungry crowd (Matthew 14:16–19).

Jesus's followers didn't multiply the food, He did. They didn't add to it, they simply passed out what He provided.

I could do that. I could dispense.

So can you.

Is there someone within your life's reach who doesn't know that God loves him? Take what you have, and break it into bite-size pieces. Divide God's love letter, and share it with a hungry, aching soul.

Pass the basket, please.

Thank You, Lord, for involving us in Your work. Help us share what You have given so abundantly. Amen.

> "But sanctify the Lord God in your hearts,
> and always be ready to give a defense
> to everyone who asks you
> a reason for the hope that is in you,
> with meekness and fear."
> 1 Peter 3:15

Day Eighty-Five

Face to Face Love

"Draw near to God and He will draw near to you."
James 4:8

*H*ave you ever watched a parent hold their child close—nose-hole to nose-hole, as my mother used to say. It's as if they are pouring in their love. Eye to eye. Face to face.

Maybe you've even done it yourself.

Holding a child close to our face is often symbolic for how we hold them close to our heart.

As an earthly parent adores the child of his love and holds her close to his face and heart, so the Lord adores us and draws us near if we let Him.

The psalmist wrote of God's people and His victories on their behalf:

"For they did not gain possession of the land by their
own sword.
Nor did their own arm save them; but it was Your
right hand, Your arm,
and the light of Your countenance, because You
favored them."
(Psalm 44:3)

See the progression? Closer and closer, from hand to arm to face.

Many times we've seen God's hand at work in our lives, providing for and protecting us. We've even seen the strength of His arm when He delivers us in miraculous ways. But have we let Him draw us so close that we see the light of His face?

The better question may be, have we drawn close enough to Him?

Oh Lord, how amazing is Your love that You would draw us close. Thank You for such intimacy. Amen.

> "For now we see in a mirror, dimly,
> but then face to face.
> Now I know in part,
> but then I shall know just as I also am known."
> 1 Corinthians 13:12

DAY EIGHTY-SIX

STICKS AND STONES AND WORDS

*"Death and life are in the power of the tongue,
and those who love it will eat its fruit."*
Proverbs 18:21

We've all heard the old saying: "Sticks and stones may break my bones, but words will never hurt me."

It's a big fat lie.

I make my living with words, lining them up in just the right order and teaching workshop students to do the same. Sometimes I pass out a survey at the beginning of the class that helps me get to know people better and see how they use words.

Survey questions include:

"What's your greatest weakness when it comes to writing?"

"If you could travel back in time to witness a historical event, which one would you choose?"

"If you could take back one sentence you've spoken, what would it be?"

That last question is always a gut-buster. In the anonymity of a writing course, people tend to be honest. They write from their soul, and truth leaks out through the cracks in their answers.

"I quit."

"I wish you were dead."

"I'll buy it."

"I will never amount to anything."

"I don't love you."

"I can visit Grandma tomorrow. She'll still be there."

She wasn't.

Of all the answers to this question over the years, the most often repeated has been, "I hate you." Sometimes these three words were directed at a spouse or a friend, often to a parent. Regardless of the recipient, they always left a festering wound, doing more harm to the speaker than to the object of their anger.

Somewhere down deep inside us, we regret hateful words uttered in the proverbial heat of the moment. We instinctively know they carry enough weight to break a spirit.

And we know the old adage should really say, "Sticks and stones may break my bones, but words can crush my soul."

Words are more like stones than we think. Hurtful words can pile up and weigh a person down. Helpful words can lay a strong, supportive foundation.

Lord, help me choose my words wisely, remembering that they may stay with a person the rest of their life. Amen.

> "A wholesome tongue is a tree of life,

but perverseness in it breaks the spirit."
Proverbs 15:4

DAY EIGHTY-SEVEN

WINDOWS

*"But he who looks into the perfect law of liberty
and continues in it,
and is not a forgetful hearer but a doer of the work,
this one will be blessed in what he does."*
James 1:25

A famous singer once described television as a box with a window in it—a one-way window with people looking in but no one looking out.

I have one of those windows in my living room, and another very similar window on my desk. In fact, I have many windows on my desk via a computer system of the same name that allows me to see more than one place at one time. Thanks to technology and cameras, people today can also look back at me from that window, unlike early television.

However, I prefer the window *above* my desk through which I can see a portion of the living world where greening trees announce a coming spring.

Sometimes I sit for long uninterrupted moments taking in the view, exploring from a distance the gentle roll of neighboring hills, or the noisy rising of Canada geese from the nearby pond. It's the constancy of life that draws my gaze outside, and it calms me during otherwise tedious hours of chasing black words across the white window of my computer screen. And it calms me immeasurably more than whatever happens to be on the television in the other room.

But the window that gives something in return, even more than the pastoral setting of my surroundings, is God's Word. When I look into that window, I find out who I am and where I'm going. I see the One who loves me like no other can. I see a pathway ahead that, should I choose it, will take me into His very presence. And I find deeper peace than even the most beautiful of earthly settings can offer.

Not everyone has a breath-taking view out a picture window. Many do, yet they rarely take the time to drink it in. But everyone can get a copy of the Bible today, whether in print or online.

Regardless of your situation, make the choice to look through the window of God's Word to find your way. Unlike the people on television and the internet, He is there looking back at you, even without a camera, waiting for you to join Him.

Timeless God, You have not been, nor will You ever be, limited by technology or man's inventions. Thank You for making Yourself known to us through Your Word and the presence of Your Holy Spirit. Amen.

> "Looking unto Jesus, the author
> and finisher of our faith."
> Hebrews 12:2

Day Eighty-Eight

The Power of Scent

> "And walk in love,
> as Christ also has loved us
> and given Himself for us,
> an offering and a sacrifice to God
> for a sweet-smelling aroma."
> Ephesians 5:2

If someone came up to me and said I smelled, my reaction would depend on what they said I smelled like. Cinnamon rolls? Fresh flowers? Bacon grease, dirty socks?

People care about how they smell, and because of that, smell is big business. Air fresheners, scented candles, perfumes, and even aroma therapy are proof.

As an author, I want to fill my stories with sensory detail, especially smell, since it is the most connective of the senses. What memories surface when you read the following words?

    Hospitals
    Bakery

Tire shop
School cafeteria

The smell of diesel takes me back to our cross-country travels when we rodeoed all summer. And at the pungent scent of wet leaves, I'm a child again in my father's California walnut orchard.

Considering the variety of smells in creation, God must appreciate the power of scent.

Our olfactory nerves trigger memory quicker than visual reminders, so it is no wonder He gave specific instructions in the Old Testament for the mixing and burning of incense. Even today, frankincense and spices are used in some church services as a form of worship.

The psalmist David wrote, "LORD, I cry out to You; make haste to me! Give ear to my voice when I cry out to You. Let my prayer be set before You as incense, the lifting up of my hands as the evening sacrifice" (Psalm 141:1–2).

In Revelation 8:3 we read, "Then another angel, having a golden censer, came and stood at the altar. And he was given much incense, that he should offer it with the prayers of all the saints upon the golden altar which was before the throne. And the smoke of the incense, with the prayers of the saints, ascended before God from the angel's hand."

In the same way we take on the smell of smoke from a campfire or a hint of fragrance from a heavy-handed perfume wearer, I wonder if we take on the scent of worship when we offer praise to God.

Do I ever smell like worship? Or do I give off a distasteful odor of complaint? I wonder—what do I smell like to Him?

Oh Lord, regardless of what is happening in my life, You are worthy of my praise. May it be a sweet-smelling sacrifice to You. Amen.

> "For we are to God the fragrance of Christ
> among those who are being saved
> and among those who are perishing.
> To the one we are the aroma of death
> leading to death,
> and to the other the aroma of life leading to life."
> 2 Corinthians 2:15–16

DAY EIGHTY-NINE

THE ROCK AND HARD PLACE

> "Here is a place by Me,
> and you shall stand on the rock."
> Exodus 33:21

There is a spot between a rock and a hard place called a cleft: a crack, crevice, or fissure.

I've been there. Have you?

Nothing can reach me there.

Nothing but the hand of God.

That's where Moses was when desperation backed him up against the mountain.

He was arguing with God because everything he had worked for so long and hard had shattered around his feet.

He was arguing with God because things weren't going the way he planned. People had disappointed him. He had disappointed himself. Life was not good.

"You said You'd go with me—where are You?" Moses cried.

Had he forgotten the Red Sea?

"I am with you," God said.

"Prove it. Show Yourself," Moses demanded.

Did he have a death wish? No one sees the face of God and lives to tell about it.

But the pain and desperation were more than he could bear, and they pushed him to the place he needed to be.

God said, "There is a place near me where you may stand on a rock."

He hid Moses in the hard place—the cleft—and covered him with His hand. The same hand that had held a man of clay, held back the sea, and would one day hold the nails.

And as He passed by, Moses peeked out and saw the back of God.

Have you been that close to God? In the hard place? Where fear and fatalism die?

It is the sweetest place I know.

So why do I wait for pain to push me into His presence when I can choose to be in that place?

Near God.

Standing.

On a rock.

"And I will," He said, "cover you with My hand."

Oh God, cover me. Amen.

> "My Presence will go with you,
> and I will give you rest."
> Exodus 33:14

Day Ninety

The Good Shepherd

"I am the good shepherd.
The good shepherd gives His life for the sheep."
John 10:11

When I was a child, my father told me of sheepherders who drove their flocks down our county's dirt roads, walking from one hay-stubble field to the next. One day as a flock pressed along the road in front of my grandparents' farm, a stray dog ran toward the sheep. It jumped up on the backs of their closely packed bodies and began ripping and tearing into their flesh. The sheepherder worked his way through the press, grabbed the mauling dog, and killed it with his bare hands.

My grandmother had watched the whole thing and ran down her lane toward the road to see if the sheepherder was hurt. As she approached him, she saw that one of his arms had been ripped open by the dog's teeth and was bleeding freely. She offered to help him and invited him to the farmhouse, but the shepherd shook his head no.

Wrapping his bloody arm in the shirt from his back, he said, "I cannot leave my sheep," and he walked down the road with his flock.

The picture my father painted with his story reminds me of the shepherd of my soul. Jesus fought for me on the cross of Calvary, and freely poured out His blood. He gave His life in place of mine and rescued me from the dogs of despair and death.

Yet even that wasn't enough in God's perfect plan. Jesus rose from the dead to walk down the road with me every day of my life. He will never leave me.

He will never leave you either. We are His sheep.

Thank You, Lord, for dying for me and living again. Thank You for fighting for me, and for always being with me on this path of life. Amen.

> "I will never leave you nor forsake you."
> Hebrews 13:5

Learning to Look and Listen:

An Exercise in Setting the Lord Always Before Me

> "I have set the LORD always before me.
> Because He is at my right hand,
> I shall not be moved."
> Psalm 16:8

How can we learn to recognize the finger and voice of God as He underscores His Word in our lives? First, we choose to make Him the focus of our attention, just as the psalm-writer David did. Because God was as near as his right hand, he could not be moved, shaken, forced off the path, or made to waver.

Next, we ask.

Jesus said if we ask, He will answer (Luke 11:9). Do you really want to hear and see the lessons God has for you? If so, then ask Him to open your spiritual eyes and ears and get ready for Him to answer. Pay close attention to ideas or concepts that are repeated in your life. The Lord will confirm His word to you by reinforcing it through different sources. And remember that God has already set in order His plan to speak to your heart. For "since the creation of the world His invisible attributes are clearly seen, being understood by the things that are made" (Romans 1:20).

You can learn to see the words of God unfold before your eyes in your surroundings or in everyday situations. Begin by following these simple steps.

In nature:

* Find an aspect of your natural surroundings that echoes a principal from God's Word. Look at first for the obvious—the way your flowers respond to deep watering or night bugs swarming your porch light in the darkness. Write out what you see or hear or feel:

_____

_____

_____

_____

* Using a concordance or the back of a study Bible, look up a key word from what you wrote—a word like *water* or *light*, something that relates to the principle you have chosen. For example, my Bible has twenty-seven entries in the back under the word *water*; a large concordance will have many more. Don't be overwhelmed by the number of options. Just start by reading through a few of the verses listed in Psalms or Proverbs until you find one that describes the principle you are looking for.

Your word: _____
Your Scripture verse: _____

* What do you think God is saying to you through His creation?

_____

_____

_____

_____

* Do you see a parallel in His written Word? Write out the verse you have chosen and how it applies.

_____

_____

_____

_____

* Now pen a brief prayer asking God to help you apply His truth to your life, or thanking Him for blessing you in a specific way.

_____

_____

_____

_____

In circumstances or relationships:

* Is there a confrontation you are dreading, something like your least favorite relative coming for dinner? Maybe your work environment isn't all you would like it to be. Write out the situation.

_____

_____

_____

_____

* Decide on a key word or phrase that addresses your situation—a word like fear, worry, sickness, or anger. Look for it in a concordance or reference Bible and choose one of the verses listed under the word that could relate to your situation. If you can't find the exact word you want, try using a synonym—a word that means almost the same as the one you first thought of.

Your word: _____
Your verse: _____

* What could God be saying to you through these circumstances? Write out your Scripture verse and thoughts on the subject.

_____

_____

_____

_____

* Do you see a parallel between His written Word and your circumstances? Write out what you are thinking.

_____

_____

_____

_____

* Conclude with a brief prayer for help in this and similar situations and for courage to do the right thing.

_____

_____

_____

_____

_____

Finally, be patient. Wait on the Lord. Be still before Him. Let Him know that you really want to see His Word unfold before you. And praise Him for His faithfulness in revealing His heart to you!

~

Thank you for reading my devotional book, *Always Before Me.* I pray the stories were an encouragement, and if one of them touched your heart in a special way, I'd love to hear from you. You can reach me via my website contact page at www.davalynnspencer.com.

May the Lord bless you on your path with Him.

Acknowledgments

I offer my deepest love and gratitude to my family for encouraging me as a writer. Thank you to my children Jake, Amanda, and Chad, and their spouses, as well as Mary Beth Price and Cam Hamilton for allowing me to share their life experiences. Thanks also to Reverend Lon Heighton for his perusal of the final section. And countless thanks to two of my sisters in Christ: Suzie Veatch, for her faithful life and cheerfulness, and Jill Maple, for her support and ongoing encouragement. The pristine honesty, bountiful laughter, and unending prayers of these two women have helped make this book possible.

ABOUT THE AUTHOR

Davalynn Spencer's story-devotions have appeared in multiple publications including *Chicken Soup for the Soul* and Guideposts' *All God's Creatures* and *Miracles Do Happen*. She is a bestselling, multi-published author of inspirational Western romance, an award-winning former journalist, and a sought-after speaker for women's events. She makes her home along the Front Range of Colorado's Rocky Mountains.

~May all that you read be uplifting.~

www.ingramcontent.com/pod-product-compliance
Lightning Source LLC
Chambersburg PA
CBHW020525080526
44583CB00013B/736